Château Palmer

Noblesse oblige

RENÉ PIJASSOU

Château Palmer

Noblesse oblige

PHOTOGRAPHS BY
JEAN-PIERRE LAGIEWSKI

Stock

A special printing of numbered copies of this book
has been reserved for Château Palmer.
This copy is number

3 5 1 8

In the Kingdom of Margaux

An unique flowery bouquet.

Château Palmer represents one of the most prestigious duke-doms in the Kingdom of Margaux. It is recognised for the pro-duction of a wine that is round and elegant, dark ruby red in colour, with a unique flowery bouquet and a smooth flavour of exceptional finesse.

These characteristics are born of a marriage between the classic noble grape varieties of the Médoc – cabernet sauvignon, mer-lot, petit verdot and cabernet franc – and the exceptional *terroir* of the area, which combine in that mysterious alchemy that is at the root of all great wines.

The Palmer vineyard extends beyond the *commune* of Margaux, from which it derives its *appellation d'origine contrôlée*, into Issan and Cantenac. In this royal triangle alone, there are 18 classed growths, of which Château Palmer is one, having been classified as a *troisième cru* in 1855.

Why does this region produce such excellent wine? The answer lies in the geology of the area as much as in the geography.

The Palmer vines are situated at the centre of a plateau, which is formed by a series of low ridges, called *croupes*. The gently sloping surface, aided by a network of man-made drains, pro-vides excellent drainage, virtually eliminating the risk of stag-nant water – dramatically described, at the beginning of this century, by Migault-Lamothe, estate manager of Château Latour, as "the poison of the vines".

The Palmer soil covers part of the strata of *graves* (gravel) known as *Günz*, which was laid down by the Garonne more than a mil-lion and a half years ago. The *graves* are smooth, rounded pebbles mixed into sandy clay – the ancient alluvial foundations of today's terraces which were formed by huge flows of mud and subsequent soil erosion. This *Günz* strata is the foundation of all the best Médoc terroirs. As at Latour, it is the larger stones (up to 15cm) that predominate at Palmer – a mix of brittle *lydiennes*

black pebbles, white quartz and quartzite marbled with black, as well as pink, red and green stones originating from the Palassou.

Poor and infertile land.

A further condition essential for the birth of a great wine is the geological substrata. In the Médoc, this usually consists of marl, laid down during the tertiary era.

The roots of the more mature vines – many of them more than 50 years old – can burrow up to eight metres deep, seeking nourishment far into the tertiary base. Due to the predominance of quartz, the Médoc soil tends to be acid and is so poor that it is unsuitable for other crops – "A poor and infertile land", as they wrote of it in the 16th century. Before it became a great wine-growing region, the Médoc was an area of moorland and forest, producing little more than crops of rye. The founding fathers of the Médoc vineyards chose this land precisely for this reason: they wanted a low crop yield in order to produce wines of a high quality. The climate also is of decisive importance. In the Médoc, the

11

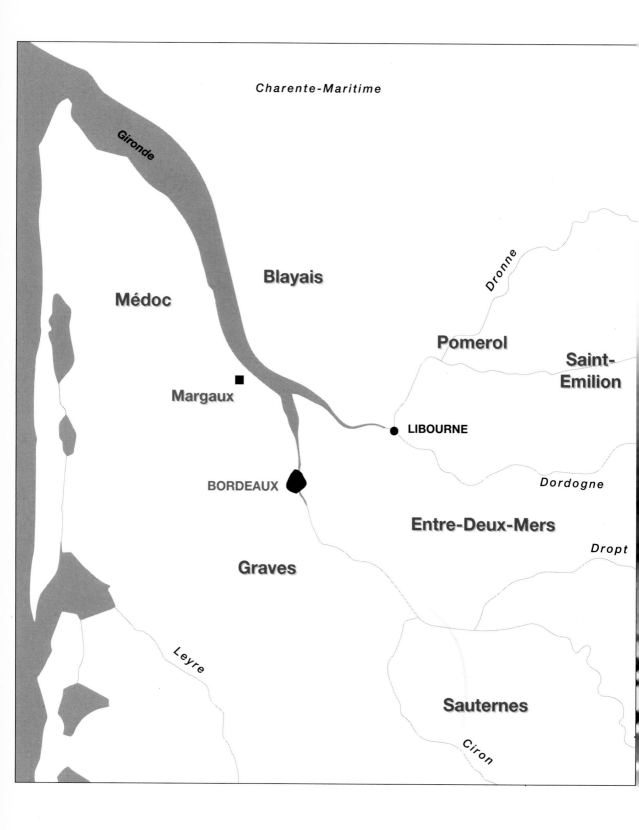

Charente-Maritime

Gironde

Blayais

Médoc

Dronne

Pomerol

Saint-
Emilion

■
Margaux

LIBOURNE

Dordogne

BORDEAUX

Entre-Deux-Mers

Dropt

Graves

Leyre

Sauternes

Ciron

summer and early autumn months are usually warm, dry and sunny. There is little rain in the spring, which tends to come early, encouraging the early flowering of the vines in May and June. The wide waters of the Garonne estuary act as a thermal regulator so that damage from late frosts is very rare, particulary for those vines planted close to the river. "Winters which kill", such as that of February 1956, are very rare. But it is also true that the Aquitaine climate can be capricious. Summer can be wet, preventing the grapes from maturing, and, at times, producing "grey rot", though modern technology now enables this to be better controlled. But poor weather at the end of the ripening period will still tend to produce wines that lack colour, and are light. There is a saying that "August makes the must", so that when the temperatures then regularly reach 30 °C, and when September is sunny, the perfect maturity that can be attained results in a great vintage. Fortunately, at Palmer particularly, the fat years outnumber the lean. Most harvests produce grapes which have the potential of being converted into a great wine, which must then be cellared, whilst time weaves its magic to complete the process, liberating all the subtle aromas of a great vintage.

Ancient Times

🌿 Birth of the Domain.

The origins of Palmer date back to the 18th century, to a small vineyard in La Palu d'Issan in Cantenac, at the time called Château de Gascq. This property belonged to an aristocratic Bordeaux family. The Gascqs were advisers to, and presidents of, the Parliament of Bordeaux. They were an illustrious family, owning further estates in Preignac-Barsac. Nearly a century before, one of their members, Jeanne de Gascq, had married Jacques de Ségur, adviser to the Bordeaux Parliament and founder of Château Lafite in Pauillac.

The basic gestures in the vineyards have not changed since the Middle Ages. (Private collection.)

During the 18th century, France was to undergo not one, but two revolutions. One is well known, the epic, political, French Revolution. The other was just as French, but less dramatic, and is less well known. This concerned the emergence of a new approach to wine making, in Bordeaux particularly. Until then, Bordeaux had produced "claret", a light wine described as "good, pure, neat, new and emminently marketable". It had been very popular with the English since the 12th century. The great medieval wines exported from France did not come from the Médoc, but were grown in the Graves of Bordeaux and along the banks of the two rivers and their common estuary. A few further vineyards were situated to the north of a stream known as the *jalle* de Blanquefort.

All this began to change in the 17th century when war was declared between Louis XIV and protestant England. The English had fired the first shot by imposing heavy taxes on French products, and in particular on wine. The traditional Gascony clarets went out of favour at this time as entrepreneurial Dutch merchants set out to introduce to the english market not only new drinks, such as herbal teas from the colonies, chocolate, coffee, tea and also new beers, rich in hops, and brandywine, but also new types of wine that became fashionable: unfortified port, white wines from Lisbon, very dark red wines produced by the vineyards of Cahors, Spain and even Italy.

❦ "Claret Lovers".

The old-fashioned clarets had to fight to compete, and before long they were in difficulties. Because prices had been raised by taxes, they had become the most expensive on the English market. Claret lovers – mostly from the upper-middle-classes – would remain loyal to the Médoc wines, but only if they were reasonably priced. Some of the wine growers were able to adapt to these conditions. One in particular, Arnaud de Pontac. First President of the Bordeaux Parliament, and owner of Château Haut-Brion at Pessac in the Graves of Bordeaux, had the bright idea of offering the English a new claret bottled under the name of his vineyard. In 1666, he sent his son to London to open a

The coopers art. From the Book of Hours of the Duchess of Burgundy. (Condé Museum, Chantilly.)

restaurant called "Chez Pontac" where the wealthy gourmets of London could taste bottles of Haut-Brion for 6 or 7 shillings. It was an excellent business strategy, appealing to the snobbish instincts of the middle-classes who would pride themselves on being able to pay extra for French wine, when Spanish and Portuguese wines could be had for a mere 2 shillings a bottle.

The rich and famous flocked to Arnaud's restaurant: Dryden, Daniel De Foe, Swift and John Locke all drank there and soon the reputation of the "new claret" was well-established. In the spring of 1677, John Locke, while staying in Bordeaux, visited M. de Pontac's vineyard and wrote the following account of the area and its soil: "such is the particular quality of M. de Pontac's vines and the soil near Bordeaux, that the wine merchants have assured me that the wine from nearby vines, although separated only by a simple ditch, and even though the soil is apparently perfectly identical, was definitely not as good". This important letter confirmed not only the reputation of Haut-Brion wine in England, but also identified, for the first time, the relevance of good soil to the winemaking process.

But a century was to pass before anyone else made the connection between wine and soil – the abbot Baurein, a well-educated and intelligent man, who instigated a survey of the vineyards of Bordeaux. Between 1784 and 1786 he published his *Variétés Bordelaises*, commenting on the growing reputation of Médoc

wines. "The demand for wines from the Médoc" he wrote "meant that people are now buying up tracts of land in this region and are keen to live there." He wrote specifically concerning Cantenac that, previously: "The Bourg wines were so well thought of in the 17th century that anyone owning an estate in both the Bourg and Médoc regions, sold their Bourg wines on the condition that the buyer agreed to also purchase their Médoc wines." This would indicate that by the time the abbot was writing the reputation of the Médoc was well on its way to being established.

Wine grower.

Abbot Baurein further explained why *la dîme* (a tax equalling one tenth of the crop) due to him by the priory of Cantenac – now Château Prieuré-Lichine – was abandoned by the abbot of Vertheuil: "because no one could have foreseen at that time (1685-1686) the popularity that wines of Cantenac, and the wines of Médoc in general would achieve".

However, in 1919, Franz Malvezin made this point: " We now believe that there may have been some confusion in names and that abbot Baurein had been writing about a wine grower from Bourgeais who was selling his wines from Saint-Androny in Bourgeais on the condition that he could sell his Cantenac wine as well. The document we saw refers to Cantenac-en-Bourgeais near Saint-Androny..."

The "New French Clarets".

Baurein's survey had failed to grasp one important fact: that, thanks to the initiative of Arnaud de Pontac, the Médoc wines, which were now sold under the impressive title of "new French Clarets", had begun to conquer the British market. English documents dating from the beginning of the 18th century,

Cooper.
Nicolas de Larmessin.
Print from late
17th Century.
(Private collection.)

Habit de Tonnellier

clearly show the improving fortunes of the great Médoc wines. A series of 153 small advertisements published in the *London Gazette* between 1703 and 1711 alerted Claret lovers to the fact that freight from French ships seized by the Royal Navy was to be sold by auction in London. One, for example, published on 6 May 1707, announced that "the English custom office wished it to be known that a recent cargo of new French prize Clarets still on their lees from Lafite, Margaux and Latour, was to be auctioned in London". These new estate wines, with which Haut-Brion wines were frequently associated, were worth five or six times more than traditional clarets. Unsurprisingly, buyers, chiefly from the ranks of the aristocracy (John Harvey, first Earl of Bristol, and the Duke of Chandos were early enthusiasts for the new wines) were easily found. But perhaps the most famous of this new breed of claret lovers was Sir Robert Walpole, the British Prime Minister. In 1733, he bought no less than 11 barrels of Médoc wines. An indication of the reputation these wines already enjoyed.

🍇 The "Planting Fury".

In 1700, the Médoc peninsula was still an area of low population and few vines. What vines there were, were planted on small pockets of land amongst the wooded areas and rye fields of the Landes. For pioneers in the wine trade, this area represented a vast space to be conquered. All the economic indicators pointed to a recovery in the financial situation: peace was imminent, the markets in North-West Europe were poised for recovery and numerous rich buyers were champing at the bit to acquire these exciting new wines. Pontac's success at Haut Brion had helped to stimulate the interest of his colleagues in the Bordeaux Parliament so that from 1700 to 1760 the area under vine was greatly increased. Other parlementarians moved in, "colonising" the Médoc, creating new vineyards and changing forever the nature of the landscape as large estates began to dominate the area. The winter of 1709, which caused widespread destruction in the Graves of Bordeaux, probably also contributed to the "planting fury" in the less-affected Médoc region. The Médoc was born.

Habit de Vigneron

Such rapid expansion caused some concern to the Royal administration. As early as 1698, Bazin de Bezons, administrator of Bordeaux, was criticising the "increasing quantity of vines" which meant a corresponding decrease in cereal production. In 1724, Claude Boucher, head of the *Généralité de Guyenne* and one of Bezon's successors, strongly criticised the "planting fury"

PREVIOUS PAGE
**The port of Bordeaux
in the 18th Century.
Painting by
Joseph Vernet.
(Maritime Museum,
Paris.)**

which seemed to have taken the proprietors of the Bordeaux region by storm.

The people of the Gironde had never been so obsessed with planting vines as they had been in the first half of the 18th century. The administrator of Bordeaux went out of his way to emphasise the perils of excess "wine growing". "Everything within a ten-league radius of Bordeaux" he lamented "has been turned into vineyards. Look out in any direction now and all you will see is row upon row of vines..."

And it was the same throughout the province. A radical solution was needed, and the Administrator had one: "all vines planted since 1709 in the 'high country' (upstream from the area controlled by the city of Bordeaux) and in the area of Bordeaux, apart from those in the Graves of the Médoc, the Graves of Bordeaux, and those of the *Costes* (hillsides) must be pulled up".

❦ An irresistible expansion.

In the end the government arrived at a wise compromise. An edict produced on 27 February 1725, stated that "express permission was needed from His Majesty for any new vines to be planted within the territory of Bordeaux". Failure to obtain permission would result in a 3,000 pounds fine.

But these repressive measures, which Claude Boucher tried to put into immediate effect, failed to overcome the tenacity and the spirit of enterprise of the Bordeaux wine-growers. It seems that he was undermined by his subordinates, in particular by delegate Jean-Pierre de Pontet, who went on to found the vineyard of Pontet-Canet. M. Tourny, Boucher's successor, sought to punish the offenders and in 1745 an investigation was initiated to discover the full scale of plantings and who had instigated them. Within three years, he had discovered 13 guilty men: the fines were levied and the illicitly planted vines were ordered to be uprooted. One of the unlucky 13 was President

Gascq, who was ordered to pull up three hectares of vines he had planted in Cantenac.

But these punishments proved to be more spectacular than they were effective and in 1756, Tourny had to admit defeat: "the fraudsters" he said "had proved more efficient that the authorities". There were now more vines than there had been in 1731. Irresistibly the vineyards continued to spread. By 1755, there

Grape picker
with his wicker hod.
18th century,
water-colour.
(Private collection.)

were vineyards established from Blanquefort to Saint-Estèphe. Estates were created: Lafite and Latour founded by the Ségur family, Margaux by Denis d'Aulède, Beychevelle by Brassier, Pichon de Longueville, Rauzan, Brane-Cantenac. With a few exceptions, all the great estates that were to be recognised in the 1855 classification were in existence.

❦ On the boats of the Gironde.

At the end of the 18th century there was no way of knowing that the modest de Gascq property would become Château Palmer. At that time the estate was still being created: the foundations were being laid for its spectacular future as a *cru classé*. By the time of the 1855 classification the vines covered 25 to 30 hectares, the old vines had been replaced with the noble varieties of Cabernet and merlot, which was introduced to the area in the first half of the 19th century. Many of the old working practices were being revolutionised.

But already in the days of de Gascq, the notion of vat selection existed. Only the most successful were used to be sold with the designation *premier vin* or *grand vin* (which was the only part of the crop to be sold with the Château name), the rest was second wine, "end of vat" and *treuillis* (from the pressings). Bottling hardly existed, so all the wine was despatched in casks by boats up the Gironde to the quays of the Chartrons, in Bordeaux.

During its maturing in both the cellars of the vineyard and those of the Bordeaux merchants, the wine received constant attention. It was frequently checked, first to make sure that the barrels were kept full, and as necessary topped up with wine from the same origin and vintage. Every three months or so the barrels were "racked", when the clean wine was separated from its deposits, and transferred to a clean cask, in which had been burned a "Dutch match" of sulphur, that sterilised both the wine and the barrel. This practice, which is essential for the preservation of

wine, dates from the 1730s, was soon generalised, and without any doubt was the most important innovation of the era.

Another technique already known was the *fouettage*, or fining. This involved beating up with a whisk made of horsehair, in a wooden basin, known as the *bontemps* (literally "good time"), whites of a dozen eggs.

These were then mixed in with the wine in the cask, forming a veil which slowly sank to the bottom, taking with it any impurities, so that the wine was left perfectly brilliant. The wine remained in the barrel for four years. This process made comparisons between the quality of the different vintages much easier, and much of the tasting jargon we know today derives from this period at the end of the 18th century.

PREVIOUS PAGE
AND ABOVE
**Château Palmer.
The traditional fining
of the wine,
using whites of eggs.**

❦ The Records of M. Lawton.

Château Palmer has its own archive – a rich and unique histori-cal record of all the sales made through the broking house of Tastet-Lawton. All of their sales of Médoc wines were recorded in this book during the second part of the 18th century, so that thanks to this diary, and to the kind cooperation of Daniel Lawton, a direct descendant of Abraham Lawton who establi-shed himself in Bordeaux in 1739, we have a comprehensive record of the then Château Gascq – its condition, its wines, and their commercial destinations. It also reveals the price hierarchy that emerged, which was to provide the basis of the 1855 classifi-cation.

Between 1746 and 1785, eleven sales and quotations refer to the Château Gascq wines, on average at a price of 462 pounds per tonneau of 900 litres. This price range puts Gascq on an equal footing with Pichon-Longueville in Pauillac but higher than

PREVIOUS PAGE,
ABOVE AND
NEXT PAGES
**Château Palmer.
Racking, which
separates the
clean wine from
the deposits which
have fallen to bottom
of the cask.**

PREVIOUS PAGE
**Château Palmer.
"Whipping":
mixing the whites of
egg into the wine.**

Lynch-Bages and Brassier, which was to become Beychevelle and whose average price was 440 pounds per tonneau. Pontet-Langoa reached 360 pounds. Château de Gascq was also at the same level as Bergeron-Ducru at Saint-Julien, the future Château Ducru-Beaucaillou, whose average price was 480 pounds. By selling his wines to the great negociant trading houses of the Chartrons, Gascq had already established for them a very honourable place in the hierarchy of fine wine.

However, the viability of the operation, in relation to the quantities being produced and the selling prices, reveals a more fragile situation. Income from the 11 recorded harvests between 1746 and 1785 grossed 80,000 pounds, a yearly income of only 7,335 pounds. When the de Gascq estate then had to withstand the rigours of the French Revolution and the ensuing Napoleonic era, it began to accumulate debts, and it was no doubt for this reason that, in 1814, that the family decided to sell to General Palmer.

But there is no reason to doubt the high quality of the wine already being made at Château de Gascq during the 18th century. It is confirmed by the prices that the wines were fetching. The broker Lawton, who was one of the first to classify wine, did not skimp in his praise for the wines of Cantenac: "one of our greatest communes" Lawton wrote. "A good vigorous wine, agreeable, with great finesse and pretty colour – light rather than full bodied. England takes the best wines. The others are part of the demand for quality wines in northern Europe and Holland. The wines of Cantenac are just as fine, and perhaps even finer, than those of Margaux, Saint Julien and Pauillac; but they are not generally as fully structured."

Lawton then continued by giving an appreciation of the different Cantenac vineyards, already identifying Château de Gascq, and mentioning that the quality of its production was considered exceptional; thus providing further evidence of the well confirmed, historic reputation of what was to become Château Palmer.

Wim van Gogh

Château Palmer

NEXT PAGE
**Grapes which will be
carefully selected.**

General Palmer

❧ The young widow and the general.

Once upon a time, General Palmer, a handsome, outgoing Englishman who loved good wine and had inherited a minor fortune, had the good luck to meet, while travelling by stagecoach from Lyon to Paris, the charming widow of a Bordeaux wine grower. She explained to him that her late husband, only recently dead, had one of the most beautiful properties anybody had seen in the Bordeaux area, and that she was on her way to Paris to dispose of her husband's estate, which would otherwise have been split up between his various heirs.

Circumstances had forced her to sell, even though such a move would mean a drastic reduction in the price. It was a beautiful property she told General Palmer, "close to Lafite, she was about to give it away to for an absurdly low price – and that she would be doing a great favour to anybody with the capital to buy it".

Legend has it that, fascinated by the plight of this beautiful young woman, the galant General offered to help her out of her financial difficulties.

By the time the stagecoach arrived in Paris, General Palmer had become the proud owner of a Bordeaux estate – and who knows if he wasn't also suggesting that they share his newly acquired domicile!

Sadly, this romantic tale, related by Captain Gronow, a contemporary of Palmer, in his Memoirs, is only a rough approximation of the truth. For one thing, Château de Gascq is nowhere near Lafite, and there is anyway no evidence that gives credit to his idyllic account. What is true, however, is the fact that Palmer did buy the Château, and extended it gradually, acquiring neighbouring lands over the years, and not by "emptying his purse", as Gronow poetically put it, "for a look which had pierced his heart".

The Château
from the vineyard.

🐛 Assembling the lands.

Having acquired his property, General Charles Palmer then
began to establish contacts amongst the wine traders and businessmen of Bordeaux. We know that he had dealings with a certain negociant, Paul Estenave, and that he bought an estate at
Cenon, situated on the right bank of the Garonne, which he also
renamed Palmer. During this time, there were many British
living in Bordeaux and the Médoc, either as merchants, trading
from the area known as the Chartrons, or running estates in the
Médoc such as Brown and Kirwan. General Palmer therefore had
access to a wide range of valuable contacts in the area. In 1814,
many estates, victims of the economic crisis forced on them by
Napoleon's Continental Blockade, were up for sale. In addition
to this, the Revolution had destroyed the great aristocratic families of the region and the businessmen of Bordeaux had moved in
to take their place: buying up some of the great châteaux and turning them into prosperous business concerns. If the confiscations
carried out during the Revolution did not in fact break up the

large estates, such as Lafite, Margaux or Beychevelle, they provided an opportunity for a number of merchants, and bankers to become proprietors of top vineyards – such as the Marquis de la Colonilla who acquired Château Margaux in 1806. Of the great estates only Latour remained, at least partly, in the hands of its original owners, the Ségurs. Lafite had been sold to three traders from Amsterdam, who acted as nominees for Vanlerberghe, a Frenchman from Douai, associated with the famous financier, Ouvrard. Château Beychevelle was bought during the Revolution by a sister of the Marquis de Brassier who had to sell it again in 1800. It was then bought by a Bordeaux ship owner, Jacques Conte, who in his turn sold it to Guestier, a famous wine merchant of the Chartrons. In 1815 Barton, another great wine merchant from Bordeaux, acquired the domain of Langoa in Saint-Julien from the Pontet family.

General Charles Palmer was clearly aware of these opportunities. When he arrived in Bordeaux with the troops of Lord Wellesley, the future Duke of Wellington, he had just come into his inheritance and apparently had sufficient credit to also buy other land in

NEXT PAGE
**The *cuvier* used at
Palmer from the times
of the Pereire until
1994.**

the Margaux area. The originality of the approach of Palmer was in the fact that he was not content with acquiring an existent wine estate, but set out to greatly expand it, by purchasing surrounding land, replanting, and creating a large domain to which to give his name. In this way he really founded an estate, as opposed to just taking over a going concern. Officially it was on the 16th of June, 1814, that he bought the Gascq domain from Marie Burnet de Ferrière, widow of Blaise-Jean-Charles-Alexandre de Gascq, for 100,000 francs, plus an annual payment of 500 litres of wine for the rest of her life. He paid a 60,000 francs deposit on the property, but, due to problems linked to the succession of Mme de Gascq, who died in 1826, the General did not make the final payment of his debt until 1835. In fact Mme de Gascq and her husband had separated in 1790 and in September of that year, and in August 1791, after a lengthy litigation with the heirs, she had acquired the de Gascq estate in her own name.

It was already an important wine growing property which included a main house, accommodation for the workers, courtyards, sheds, cellars, vat rooms, gardens, orchards, vineyards and the grazing rights of the adjoining communal fields. The estate stretched from the parish of Cantenac, where the buildings were situated, into the Parish of Margaux. It comprised around 60 hectares of land, of which half was given over to vines. The lack of legal documents relating to the sale means that it is difficult to establish the exact extent of the estate, but it is clear that it formed the heart of what was to become the General's domain.

In 1816 he bought the la Raze domain in Cantenac, followed swiftly by the Belair estate which overlapped the Cantenac-Margaux boundary. Later the following year he bought the Raucaud estate. Within three years, the Englishman had invested 212,000 francs in property and vines, that is over half the worth of his future estate. And he did not stop there. Between 1820 and 1831 he bought many buildings and workshops and continued to buy parcels of Landes country, clearing the moorland

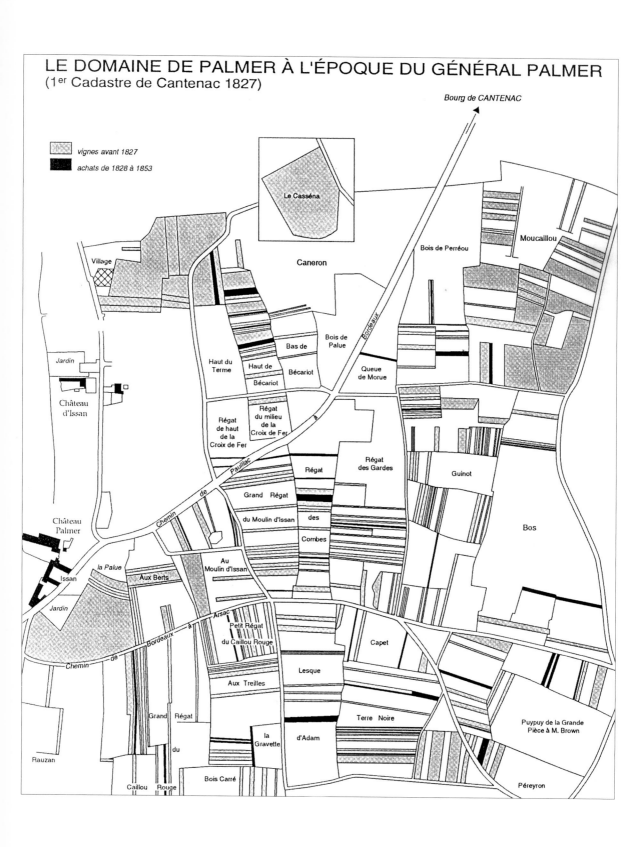

LE DOMAINE DE PALMER À L'ÉPOQUE DU GÉNÉRAL PALMER
(1er Cadastre de Cantenac 1827)

Bourg de CANTENAC

vignes avant 1827
achats de 1828 à 1853

Le Casséna

Village

Caneron

Bois de Perréou

Moucaillou

Jardin

Bois de Palue

Bordeaux

Château d'Issan

Haut du Terme

Haut de Bécariot

Bas de Bécariot

Queue de Morue

Régat de haut de la Croix de Fer

Régat du milieu de la Croix de Fer

à

Pauillac

Régat

Régat des Gardes

Guinot

de

Château Palmer

Chemin

Grand Régat du Moulin d'Issan

des

Combes

Bos

Issan

la Palue

Aux Berts

Au Moulin d'Issan

Jardin

Arsac

à

Petit Régat du Caillou Rouge

Capet

Bordeaux

de

Lesque

Chemin

Aux Treilles

Terre Noire

Puypuy de la Grande Pièce à M. Brown

Grand Régat

la Gravette

d'Adam

Rauzan

du

Caillou Rouge

Bois Carré

Péreyron

PREVIOUS PAGE
**Plan of the Palmer
domain at the time
of General Palmer.
(From the first
cadastre survey
of Cantenac,
in 1827.)**

that would constitute the vineyard known as Boston. He took over the estates of Monbrun and Jean Fort and eventually laid his hands on the extensive fields of Rondeau in Cantenac.

Within 17 years, he had spent 371,000 francs, occasionally borrowing to finance his more ambitious plans, but in the 1830s his credit in Bordeaux was still intact. When he had finished, his domain – the largest in Cantenac – comprised around 163 hectares and was a perfect example of concentrated property buying, achieved at the expense of the French aristocracy whose vast estates had been left virtually in ruins by the Revolution, and smaller bourgeois landowners, whose properties were badly run, or who had fallen on difficult times... His property could now bear comparison to his great neighbour, Château Margaux. Everything was now in place for the creation of a *grand cru classé*.

A modern entrepreneur.

The vineyard itself, covered 82 hectares and consisted of two large wine-growing units separated by 4 kms. The large vineyard surrounded the house at the centre of the estate in Issan. This part of the estate was cultivated by 20 experienced job workers (the *prix-faiteurs*) which was a mark of its size. In comparison, at that time the Latour Château employed only 14 vinetenders. The General did not skimp on his equipment, either. He had built an excellent vat room containing 15 oak vats bound in iron which could accomodate 73 hectolitres each and thus could deal comfortably with a harvest of more than 1000 hectolitres. It was clear that the Englishman did things on a grand scale. Palmer had further invested in 3 presses (*fouloirs*), 3 large tubs (*gargouilles*) encircled in wood and 16 small vats (*cuveaux*) to carry the harvest and a wheeled ladder, up which the grapes were carried to be tipped into the fermenting vats. To which must also be added large wooden buckets bound in metal (*comportes*), to carry the harvest, funnels, and metal bound wood recipients that were used for

measuring the quantities of wine when it was taken from the vats and transferred to the new oak barrels. Another interesting point is that whilst most vineyards at that time used oxen to draw the ploughs, Palmer already used horses.

Since Palmer lived in London, he could not personally oversee the running of his property. If Captain Gronow is to be believed, he

was fully aware of his "*inaptitude* at wine-growing" and consequently confided in an "active business agent", who was also a Londoner, Mr Gray, though he too was considered to be more social than competent. Nobody knows if it is true, as it has been suggested, that it was his bad advice that caused Palmer to make hazardous investments that proved disastrous, but it does seem to

Hatchets, scythes, hammers, saws and taps.

be true that Gray had many excellent contacts, was a good sales-man, and was able to sell the General's wine to a wide clientele of wealthy enthusiasts. "Palmer's claret" became sought after in the London clubs. Gray and Palmer even had the favour of the Prince Regent, though this was sadly to turn to their disadvantage.

❦ A dinner at the Prince's.

In an attempt to promote his faithful subject's wines, the Prince Regent had organised a dinner at Carlton House in London. Amongst the guests were Lord Yarmouth, whose glowing red face and ginger locks, allied to the fact that Yarmouth was the principle town for herring imports, had earned him the nickname, Red Herring. Also present were Sir William Knighton, Sir Benjamin Bloomfield and Sir Thomas Tyrwhitt, all enthusiastic gourmets.

General Palmer's wines were duly served and judged to be excellent. The Prince Regent was pleased and declared himself charmed by the wine's bouquet, which he compared favourably to a kiss. Lord Yarmouth alone remained strangely silent and when asked why, replied that when dining at the Royal table he was usually offered a different claret – and one that was infinitely preferable to this one. The wine he referred to was supplied by Carbonnel. The prince immediately asked for a bottle to be brought, so that the two could be compared. This was done, together with some anchovy sandwiches, against which it would be difficult for any delicate wine to defend itself. Perhaps the Carbonel had been prepared, like most wines at the time, specifically for the London market: probably blended with Hermitage, to give it the body that better suited to the English taste than the "delicate bouquet of the Claret" that the Prince and his companions had just finished. Unluckily for Palmer, the Prince agreed with Red Herring and declared the Carbonnel wine superior. He even went so far as to suggest to Palmer that he should make some experiments in his vineyard in order to try to produce "a better wine".

Château Palmer cellar and coopering tools.

Palmer left Carlton House a broken man. Trying to console him, Sir Thomas Tyrwhitt said that the taste of the wine had been altered by the strong flavour of the anchovies, but, in a voice loud enough to be heard by Lord Yarmouth, the General loudly retorted that it was all the fault of "that damned Red Herring". According to Gronow, the argument was settled by a duel between Palmer and Yarmouth, the outcome of which is unfortunately not recorded. To make wine suitable for the English market, claret at the time generally was blended with the fuller bodied wines of Hermitage, or Benicarlo from Spain, so this little anecdote is not completely without foundation. But what seem unlikely is that Palmer, as Gronow goes on to suggest, acting on the rather dubious advice of his Prince, uprooted all his old vines and planted new ones - all with disastrous results. As Gronows light hearted memoirs are the only source of information on this incident, it is probably wise to take none of it seriously.

❦ Organisation of the work at Palmer.

On the other hand we do have a good idea of how the vineyard of Château Palmer was run at that time. The general had entrusted

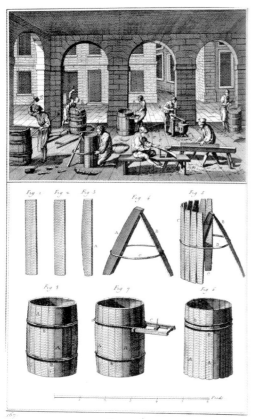

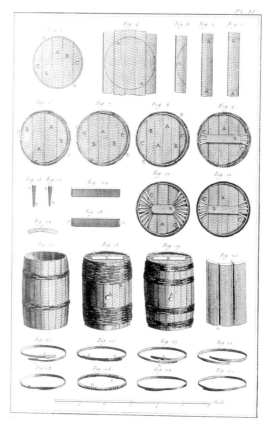

Tonnelier   *Tonnelier*

From the
"Encyclopaedia"
of Diderot and
d'Alembert (1762).

his Médoc interests to a resident Bordeaux merchant, Paul Estenave, who had succeeded a M. Belloguet. Work on the estate was administrated by Jean Lagunegrand, a Cantenac man who was responsible for a team of 40 to 50 people. Whether or not he was competent, or honest, is open to question. He was left entirely in charge, while the owner was far away in another country, and we have no idea how often he visited his estate. In view of the high overhead, the financial health of the vineyard depended on the right balance between grape yield and the selling price of the wine. Unfortunately prices for on the wines never seemed to be sufficient to bring in a profit. During the first decade for which records are available, from 1831-40, production

was low and economic
conditions did not favour
exports.   In spite of the
good yields of the "Three
Glorious" years, of 1836,
1837 and 1840, and a level
price that was appreciably
higher than it had been
during the previous century, it
seems that one had difficulty
in covering costs.   1831 had
been a disastrous year for all
the grands crus of the Médoc
even though it suited the taste of the British
market who loved strong-coloured, full-
bodied wines.   Hail storms in 1833 resulted in
wines that were green, 1835 was judged to have no
class and 1838 was bitter, and harsh.

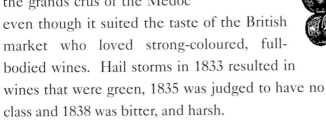

During the following decade, 1841-50, the first three years have to
be separated from the rest, as they are the last years to be produced under the aegis of General Palmer: by 1843 he had sold his
estate. The 1841 vintage was both abundant and of excellent quality. In December, Lawton gave a favourable judgement: "the red
wines of the last harvest have a very good colour" he wrote:
"They have a good taste, perfectly frank and neat and are not marked by acidity. They are more full bodied than previous years, but
at this stage they are all a little closed." He added: "We certainly
have in the red wines of 1841 all the qualities of a great year, and
even if the current firmness persists and they remain closed, we
think we will still be able to present them as very good wines, and
suitable for certain markets."

Château Palmer took full advantage of these remarks: the harvest
was sold for 1,650 francs per tonneau *en primeur* (soon after it
had been made); the highest price for a long time. Many of its

One of the lanes
at the Château.

competitors did less well. The second growths, including Mouton, were being quoted at only 1,400 francs. Latour was making 1,800 and only Lafite managed the exploit of selling 105 tonneaux at 5,500 francs, but by holding it until April 1844. The 1842 harvest was poor in quality and low in quantity. In October, Tastet, a broker, noted that he "found the wines had very little taste. They are light and agreeable, it is true, but the taste and colour is weak. I have some hopes, but fear the worst". Lawton persisted in his bad opinion, and in the end neither brokers or merchants were impressed with the new wines. Prices inevitably fell. Château Palmer sold its 1842 harvest for the modest price of 625 francs. Others managed to do better, but that was often due to late sales taking place up to two to four years afterwards. The trend for weak vintages continued in 1843 with a harvest that was disappointing on all levels: small in volume and bad in quality. Judgements were sombre: "I find some acidity and very little body" wrote Tastet. Law-

PREVIOUS PAGE
The *Esquives*,
or bungs that are
placed at the end
of the barrels
are wrapped with
rush, to provide
a tight fit.

ton thought the wines were simply "bad". Looking through the quotations for this period seems to indicate that the scale of values had disappeared. Château Palmer's meagre 1843 harvest was not sold until 1847 for the low price of 450 per tonneau. Only Château Margaux reached 1,000 francs in 1848. Lafite was quoted 800 francs and Mouton 600. In the end, as usual, failed vintages reduced everybody to the same level.

Grandeur and decline.

It was in these circumstances that Bordeaux was to learn that General Palmer had become bankrupt. Looking through the legal documents of 1843-44 the extent of his debts becomes evident. The number of his creditors had continued to increase. Amongst them, and perhaps the most daunting was the Caisse hypothécaire de Paris, a building society. The General had incurred many outstanding loans and the low income from his Médoc Château was simply not sufficient to cover them. After the dinner at the Prince Regent's, could he have embarked on an expensive programme of experiments, as had been suggested? Or was bad advice from Gray, his London manager, the cause of his downfall? Whatever the reason the General was forced to turn to usurers and life insurance schemes to find some money to pay off his debts. According to legal archives in Bordeaux, on 26 March 1834, even Palmer's wife, Mary Elizabeth Atkins, took out a mortgage charge on the Palmer estate following a judgement in her favour at the Bordeaux tribunal. Palmer was ruined in England also. According to Gronow he had to sell the Bath Theatre, and the Reform Act resulted in his losing his seat in Parliament. There was a plan launched to raise money to save him from bankruptcy, but, according to Gronow, he preferred to end his days in poverty. He was taken to court and sued for insolvency. Thus ended the wine growing career of General Palmer, but, as the man collapsed, his estate was born again.

The Pereire Saga

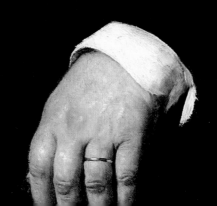

PREVIOUS PAGES
LEFT
Émile Pereire.
(Private collection.)

RIGHT
Isaac Pereire.
Painting by Bonnat,
1878. *(Museum of the*
Château of Versailles.)

A Painful Transition.

Despite being in a critical situation, the Palmer estate was much coveted. Once the founder had disappeared from the scene, a legal battle was opened.

Paul Estenave, a former Bordeaux merchant, acting as agent for Palmer, sold the estate to Demoiselle Françoise-Marie Bergerac on 12 January 1843. The sale price was 284,400 francs including 10,400 which was owed to Jean Lagunegrande, business administrator for the General. Thus the estate had been valued at 274,000 francs net. If compared to the total sums recently invested it shows the General to have made a 26 per cent loss on his property, and perhaps indicated the fundamental reason for his failure.

Estenave and Mlle Bergerac were in fact living together as man and wife in Bordeaux, where Françoise-Marie Bergerac was described as a "proprietor, of independant means with no profession". It seems possible that in order to retain the property for the General, Paul Estenave had used her name as a nominee, but nobody knows if this was so.

On the 28 April 1843, in accordance with the law, Mlle Bergerac notified the creditors of her acquisition of the estate. Amongst these were the Paris-based building society who made a higher bid for the property, which the Tribunal of 1st Instance of Bordeaux declared valid. Bergerac, no doubt prompted by Estenave, appealed against the decision on the grounds that the property had anyway been sequestered. But on the 3rd of January 1844 the Royal court of Bordeaux declared the appeal non receivable and ordered the sale of the Château by auction to take place on 29 January 1844. Palmer was sold to the Caisse hypothécaire for 312,840 francs and remained in their hands for the next ten years.

Details of the Château administration during this time are unclear but what is known is that the sale of the 1843 harvest showed a large deficit and from then until 1853, the Palmer

harvests were minimal in volume. The yearly average reached 62 tonneaux, 550 hectolitres from 80 hectares of vines – a slight drop compared to the previous era. No harvest reached 100 tonneaux, though the quantities ranged from 90 in 1847 to only 30 in 1853 when the first symptoms of oidium, the "disease of the vine" began to show. The average selling price of the six years that we have been able to trace during this period was approximately 818 francs – an honourable result, but one that does not take into account the fact that sales figures from the other four years are missing. The maximum price obtained was for the 1851 harvest when a total sales value of 120,000 francs was reached.

In 1844, the year when the Caisse hypothécaire took over the ownership of the Château, the production volumes of the entire Cantenac Margaux area remained average, unlike the rest of the

Château Palmer.
Casks aligned
in the cellar reserved
for the new wine.

Roses at the end of
the rows of vines
can provide an
indication that a risk
of oidium is imminent.

Médoc which achieved much more plentiful harvests. At
Palmer, only 60 tonneaux were produced. Lawton noted that it
was "appreciated" as a *très grande année* at first but then rejudged
it as "good only". But it was good in comparison with previous
harvest and excited enthusiasm in Bordeaux. Here is Tastet on
the subject, writing on 18 November 1844: "It is almost super-
fluous to mention the wines of the last harvest of 1844. The
importance and promptness of the purchases, the prices paid for
the *vin classé* show a favourable impression after the tastings
organised since the harvest... The successful Médoc wines show
an intense and brilliant colour, great warmth, a good bouquet
and a distinguished taste, neat and fine. They show great class.

In fact, all the communes presented successful wines; Cantenac, Margaux, Saint-Julien and Pauillac are exceptionally distinguished."

Prices rose dramatically. Palmer sold its 60 tonneaux of 1844 at 1,500 francs, though not until 1849. It had not been able to take part in the *primeur* campaign, probably as a result of the change of ownership. The other Châteaux of the Médoc had sold at even higher prices in October and November 1844.

The new price level did not survive the following year due to both low production and very bad quality. The harvest was late and ruined by rain. Grey rot was rampant. In mid-December, Tastet declared: "Our 1845 red wines are lacking body and colour and have an acidity that provides the overiding characteristic of the year". Inevitably, the prices fell as dramatically as they had previously risen. Palmer sold its harvest for 310 francs per tonneau, in November 1846; the lowest price in its whole history. The other Châteaux did not do much better.

❧ Oidium.

In 1852, the whole of the Médoc was affected by oidium. Lawton noted that "the very real fears that we have for our vineyards next year due to this menacing disease have had almost no affect on the buying and selling of the wines – as business decisions had already been made".

The small volume of the 1853 vintage was due to oidium. Palmer produced only 30 tonneaux of great wine. The Tastet-Lawton office mentioned the "violence" of the attack of the oidium in certain areas: "the frequent rains both helped the disease to develop and impeded the maturation of the grapes, so the harvest still had to be gathered even though the level of maturity was not generally satisfactory." In the most affected parts, he added "whole harvests had been abandoned". The quality of the new vintage was not satisfactory. "The red wines

PREVIOUS PAGES
**Château Palmer.
The main entrance
for visitors is on
the south side.**

of 1853 have a medium colour and suffer from too much acidity.
They all lack body."

Such a poor vintage was difficult to sell, particularly as a classed
growth. Lawton hinted that the market in *grands vins* was about
to be drastically damaged by oidium: "The small quantity of 1853
wines, the reduced production in almost all vineyards, the likeli-
hood that the disease will spread further next year and the corresponding increased demand by consumers, means that we will be
forced to use this year's wines – despite their inferior quality."

Five other third growths were not able to sell their production
until December 1856, and even then at low prices.

Thus it was that in 1853, Médoc entered the era of oidium, and
Château Palmer changed hands once again.

❦ A french success story.

On 9 June, 1853, the Caisse hypothécaire sold Château Palmer
and its 83 hectares of vines to the Parisian bankers Émile and
Isaac Rodrigues Pereire for the sum of 419,000 francs. The
Caisse made a profit of 97,160 francs, roughly 31 per cent of its
acquisition price in 1844. All in all, a good business transaction
taking into consideration the mediocre results of the Palmer
exploitation during the last ten years, and the risks for the future
that the oidium epidemic engendered.

On 28 July, Isaac Pereire officially informed "Mary Elizabeth
Atkins, wife of Mr Charles Palmer, Major General in the service
of his British Majesty, and living in London" of his purchase of
Château Palmer. It must be remembered that General Palmer's
wife still held a mortgage on her husband's Médoc estate.

The purchase of Château Palmer by the Pereire brothers was an
economic symbol of the times. The extraordinary economic
expansion during the Second Empire created massive wealth in
the business classes; particularly amongst the banking fraternity
who centralised savings, and had the capital at their disposal to

13. MARGAUX — Château Palmer - BR - 33

Postcard from the end of the 18th century, showing the north side of the Château.

James de Rothschild, the friend, and later the rival. Photograph by Disderi. *(Carnavalet Museum, Paris.)*

PREVIOUS PAGE
**The vineyard
of Palmer, seen
from the roof
of the Château.**

finance the explosion of business opportunities. Yet the Pereire venture into the wine business was surprising. Bankers such as the Rothschilds, heirs to old and solid fortunes, would soon become Médoc owners, but the Pereires were *nouveaux riches* descendants of a Portuguese, Jewish family that had emigrated to Bordeaux in 1741. Their grandfather, Jacob, had left the memory of a generous man, particularly dedicated to the cause of the deaf and dumb. Émile was born in 1800, his brother Isaac in 1806. In 1825, the brothers, young and poor, moved to Paris and found employment as clerks at the Rothschild bank, at the time directed by Baron James de Rothschild. They became involved with the saint-simonien movement, which strongly influenced their business and humanitarian philosophies. Soon they were to be seen on the floor of the Stock Exchange, infiltrating the business world of the July Monarchy. At the same time they found time to write numerous articles in the Paris press about financial matters, supporting new financial policies, based on lower rates of interest than those being applied by the Bank of France. Then they turned their attention to the new form of transport, the railways. In 1835, Louis-Philippe granted them the concession for a line from Paris to Saint-Germain-en-Laye. Together with the Rothschilds, they formed a company which ran the line and Émile became the director of the first railway company to exist in France. The line was inaugurated in August 1837, and in 1842 the Gare Saint-Lazare was opened to the public.

The Pereire passion for railways did not cease there: with the introduction of the railway charter in June 1842, their involvement increased considerably, and in 1845 the Rothschilds were also given the concession for the railway Compagnie du Nord; before long Émile was at its head.

During the first years of the Second Empire, though the Pereires failed to become involved in the PLM line (Paris-Lyon-Marseille), which was in the hands of Paulin Talabot, they became the uncontested masters of the Compagnie du Midi,

Medallion above one of the doors, with the initials of Isaac Pereire.

which created the line from Bordeaux to Bayonne, and Bordeaux to La Teste, that was then extended as far as the summer resort of Arcachon, which was virtually their creation. As a result of the 1848 revolution, the Prince-President Louis-Napoléon Bonaparte, later Napoléon III, came to power. The Pereires, unlike the Rothschilds, gave him immediate enthusiastic support, which put them in a strong position to create their own financial empire. By 1869, their fortune was estimated at 200 million gold francs – greater than that of James de Rothschild! The heart of their empire was the Société Générale du Crédit Mobilier which enjoyed the full backing of the new regime. The basis of the Pereire success lay in the fact that they had managed to pioneer a new kind of saving – one geared to the needs of small investors as well as commercial and industrial enterprises, allying themselves to all those who wanted to create a counterweight to the traditional Orleanist banks. Baron James de Rothschild haughtily refused to have anything to do with the new venture, causing a rift between the two families and the start of their rivalry.

As well as the railways, the Pereire brothers were active in property, supporting the urban regeneration engineered by Hausmann, acquiring land, building and hotels particularly in the XVIIth arrondissement. They also participated in the renovation of Marseille.

🦋 Palmer sardines!

In 1861, the brothers founded the Companie générale trans-atlantique and started to be involved in shipping.

Through this they became interested in dockside activites and bought two bankrupt Concarneau canning factories, creating a new sardine canning factory at la Croix which they named Palmer.

As an incongruous consequence to this, both the *grands vins* of Cantenac and the sardines from the factory at Concarneau were sold under the same name: Palmer.

The brothers' interest in the Château Palmer must have derived from their Bordeaux origins and their fortuitous acquisitions on the Atlantic coast.

It was a tiny drop in the ocean of their fortune, but it also fitted in well with one of their other obsessions: the cultivation of the Landes in Gascony.

Separately from the resort at Arcachon, where the Pereires owned the famous chalet Pereire, 16 villas and two vast domains that were to become le Parc Pereire, as well as a casino, Émile had, in 1852, bought roughly 9,000 hectares of *landes*, situated within four communes close to the bay of Arcachon: Lanton, Audenge, Biganos and Mios.

This vast area of uncultivated land was sold to them by Count de Tracy, the countess de Clermont-Tonnerre and Madame d'Equevilly, who seem to have concluded a rewarding sale. Not long afterwards, the brothers purchased the domain of the Coq in Sainte-Eulalie-en-Born, south of lake Parentis.

In 1857, they increased their *landes* holdings by 2,000 hectares at Teich bringing the total extent of their property up to 11,000 hectares, a size comparable to the Imperial domain of Solférino!

In 1858, in order to administer their forest lands, the brothers created the Pereire Society, with a working capital of 18 million francs.

Arcachon and its pine forest, whose healthy air is particularly beneficial to asthmatics, such as Émile Pereire... *(Private collection.)*

The Pereire at Palmer.

The two businessmen were in love with the Bordeaux region, with Arcachon and its glorious pine forests. Its good clean air was a boon to Emile, who suffered from asthma and this must have been a major factor in their decision to buy a château and a cellar in the Médoc.

For Émile, Palmer was a chance to escape the formality of his life at the faubourg Saint-Honoré in Paris and the tensions at his château d'Armanvilliers near the Rothschilds at Ferrière.

By chance or not, the rivalry between the Pereires and the Rothschilds was to be carried to the Médoc. On 10th March 1853, just a week before Emile Pereire was to start negotiations with the Caisse hypothécaire of Paris to buy Château Palmer, Baron Nathaniel de Rothschild, from London, had bought Mouton, in Pauillac. The Paris Rothschild bank continued to manage what was to become Château Mouton-Rothschild, until the 1870s. In 1868, Baron James Rothschild was also to establish himself at Pauillac, when he purchased Château Lafite for the considerable

price of 4,800,000 francs. So the ferocious rivalry betwen the two families continued.

❦ A distinguished vineyard.

Isaac and Émile Pereire's first step was to build a new house at Palmer: a more comfortable residence than the original master house. They employed an architect from Bordeaux, Burguet, to build the present château which was set on the Bordeaux to Pauillac road. It was to be a simple two-storeyed building with a cone-shaped tower at each of the four corners. Slate roofs and two rows of high, mullioned windows, small skylights and glass doors opening out from the salons of the ground floor completed the picture. Carved into the stone lintels were historic medallions entwined with vine leaves and bunches of grapes, bearing the initials of the château's new owners. The château itself is surrounded by lawns and flower beds. The courtyard in front of the main aspect of the house is formed by a grassy area planted with trees. Unfortunately, following a sale of the contents

Château Palmer.
The dovecote,
in the Château
courtyard.

NEXT PAGE
A door in
the west turret.

of the house in 1938, no record of the 19th century furnishings remains.

The initial impact of the house is one of elegance and charm. In his 1867 book describing the *grands crus* of Bordeaux, Alfred Danflou mentioned "the beautiful facade of Palmer, so charming and gracious that it reminds you of the villas that border Lake Como. Visit Palmer" he went on "and you will surely agree: here is a house worthy of such a *grand vin*". The Pereire brothers had graced a distinguished vineyard with an exceptional château.

By 1853, the Pereires were busy reorganising the house and had begun work on the restoration of the vineyard. They employed a new estate manager, a M. Lefort, an experienced technician who was famous for his expertise in wine-growing and oenology. He had been mentioned by the broker Armand Tastet in his 1867 report on Pontet-Canet as being one of the most experienced wine growers in the Médoc.

It seems likely that he had to undertake to repair the damage that had been done in the vineyard, both by the negligence of the previous owner, and by the ravages of disease. The Pereire brothers

PREVIOUS PAGE
TOP
The "Pereire", one
of the first long
distance steamships.
(Private collection.)

BELOW
One of the great
creations of the
Pereires : the dining
room of the Hôtel
du Louvre.
(Private collection.)

had guaranteed the future survival of Palmer by including it in the Société Civile Universelle Pereire so that after the death of Émile in 1875, and that of Isaac in 1880, the family maintained this company until it was finally wound up in 1938, when the Château was sold.

The vineyard was improved throughout this time by the acquisition of parcels of land from the surrounding areas, in particular at Brauzes. The most important purchase was made in 1890, when the 34 hectares Port-Aubin property in Cantenac became part of the Palmer estate. Port-Aubin was planted with 28 hectares of vines, but it was lower lying inferior land so that its production was not sold under the Palmer label.

It seems that during the same period the plots known as Solles were also acquired and planted. During the 1920s, the Palmer domain extended over 190 hectares, of which 120 hectares were planted with vines. By then Palmer was the largest vineyard in Cantenac-Margaux. In June 1932, the Société civile Pereire acquired five more parcels of land, previously owned by Boyd-Cantenac, adding a further 16 ares to the estate.

According to the Pereire's biographer, Jean Autin, Émile loved Palmer and visited it often, particularly during the years 1868-70. After the partial bankruptcy of the Crédit mobilier in 1867 and the collapse of many other Pereire concerns that same year, Émile and his family moved more or less permanently to Arcachon so that he could be near his Château. The Pereire family as a whole were attached to their vineyard and in spite of the forced sale of many of their Paris assets they retained Palmer until 1938.

❦ The Great Crisis.

Until 1860 Palmer suffered from the full impact of oidium, which had affected the vines even more severely as a result of the fact that the vineyard was in the process of being restored. Powerless to prevent its progress, the wine growers of Cantenac

Château Palmer.
The "chestnut"
courtyard.

had, for the last ten years or so, watched helplessly as their harvests gradually diminished. In Médoc, it is estimated that at least two out of every five harvests were lost to oidium.

At Palmer, only 240 tonneaux were produced between 1853 and 1860 – a yearly average of 30 tonneaux. This represented 42.5 % of the yearly average for the previous decade. The smallest harvest occurred in 1856, when a mere 11 tonneaux of *grand vin* were made. The yield per hectare was nugatory, though later it did improve to some degree. 78 tonneaux were produced in 1858, though the total fell again to 58 tonneaux in 1860. These two years suffered less because the summers were hot and dry, providing less favourable conditions for the fungus to develop.

For two or three years the wine growers were totally distraught. The various treatments recommended, often farfetched, had no effect. But from 1855 the real solution, spraying with sulphur, was developed by certain properties, such as Giscours at

Labarde, and Lagrange at Saint-Julien which belonged to Comte Duchâtel. Yet until the 1860s most producers were reluctant to use this "flower of sulphur" on their vines. Such an attitude was probably encouraged by the fears of the negociants and brokers in Bordeaux who argued that such a practice would give the wine a "sulphury taste". The wines of Lagrange were judged bad because they "smelled of sulphur". If, little by little, opinions changed and from 1860 onwards, the use of sulphur on the vines became common practice, much time and money had been lost in the meantime.

A completely unexpected consequence of all this, was the increase in prices for the *grands vins*. Demand for the fashionable Médoc wines, now in short supply, was so great in Britain, that wine lovers were prepared to pay almost any price to get a share of the rare quantities available. Merchants, and owners, naturally took advantage of the situation and began pushing prices up as far as they would go. The Second Empire's free

Château Palmer.
The "clock wing"
of the Château.

trade policy, which resulted in lower rates of duty, also helped. Returning to the modest harvest in 1854 and the beginning of this new era, Lawton wrote that: "The quality wines of Médoc have a very bright and beautiful colour; their taste is mature: fine and distinguished and they hold promise of developing a generous bouquet." The volume was not great, but it was a fine vintage all the same.

The market became greatly excited. As Lawton went on to say: "The demand is everywhere. The owners are exalted, asking prices that are crazy. The quantity available is less than ever before, so purchases are being made much sooner than one would have thought. On the other hand the same reasons are making proprietors ever more difficult, so that prices are extremely high and those that still have wine to sell are asking even higher prices than those who have already sold."

Taking full advantage of this atmosphere of commercial euphoria, Palmer engineered something of a *coup* – managing to sell the

Château Palmer.
A reception room.

14 tonneaux of the harvest for 4,000 francs each, providing a revenue of 56,000 francs and easily eclipsing the other Châteaux in the Médoc. Over all, the *troisième cru* managed to achieve an excellent average price of 2,815 francs per tonneau.

❧ The 1855 classification.

It is not certain, on the other hand, that the classification of 1855 did anything to help price levels of Château Palmer. The list published on 18th April 1855 was a fairly straightforward way of making official what was already a recognised situation. Before this date many winewriters, such as Jullien, William Franck, Paguierre and Le Producteur had favoured the idea of a classification for the *grands crus* of Médoc. No one, however, had previously suggested drawing up a list quite the same as this one.

It was made at the request of the Bordeaux Chamber of Commerce who had been entrusted by an Imperial Commission to organise a presentation of the *grands vins* of Bordeaux at the Universal Exhibition of 1855. Inevitably there was both bargaining, and some intrigue. The Rothschilds, who had owned Brane-Mouton since 1853 wanted to make sure that it was classified a first growth, in order to equal its rival and neighbour, Lafite. Though this nominally belonged to Sir Samuel Scott of London, he was in fact acting as a nominee for the heirs of Vanlerbergue. In 1851 the son of Isaac Thuret, who was then owner of Mouton, had already tried to promote Mouton as a first growth, but he had been dissuaded by the manager, Lestapis, who wrote on the 24th March 1851: "Mouton, as first of the *seconds crus*, must keep its rank." And anyway the new success of Mouton was too recent for the traditional classification to be modified.

Château Palmer was placed in the third class of the Médoc *grands crus*, appearing half way down this famous document. In truth, it was the right classification. It was only two years into

the Pereire ownership, far too soon for them to have repaired ten years of neglect by the Caisse hypothécaire, or the ravages of oidium.

❧ Palmer during the *Belle Époque*.

Now that their vineyard was back in working order, the Pereire brothers were well-placed to benefit from the good revenues of the *Belle Époque* of the XIXth century that the Médoc was to enjoy. The 1860s provided a substantial improvement in production. The yearly average during this decade was 92 tonneaux and about half the harvests achieved 105 or more of *grands vins*. The richest harvest of all occured in 1869, reaching the grand total of 125 tonneaux, while the lowest total of 50 tonneaux came in 1863. The years blighted by oidium had ended. The next decade saw further increases in prosperity and the annual average production at Palmer reached 129 tonneaux, a 40 per cent increase on the previous decade. These results confirm the healthy state of the vineyard, helped no doubt by the use of fertiliser. Three harvests were particularly abundant: 1874 rose to 190 tonneaux, 1875 was the best yet – a staggering total of 245, not far off the quantities produced today. Finally the 1878 harvest also performed well. Palmer and the other *grands crus* of Médoc could now enjoy a period of prosperity and leave the miserable years of 1844 to 1853 behind them. The Médoc was enjoying its golden age.

❧ Mildew and phylloxera.

Yet from 1881 to 1890 the Médoc was to go through another difficult period: that of the phylloxera and mildew. The *Phylloxera vastarix*, a tiny insect, had first appeared in 1874, and by 1880 it could be found throughout the area, spreading everywhere and attacking the roots of the vines with slow and deadly efficiency.

The wine growers realised once again that they had no effective defences against such a virulent bug – other than to replant the vineyards, grafting onto resistant American rootstocks. But the *grands crus* took a long time to accept such a drastic solution – particularly as the merchants opposed it, fearing that it would affect the quality of the wine. So for the next quarter of a century, the Médoc *grands crus* launched a harrowing and costly battle against phylloxera with the aid of insecticides. First they injected carbon sulphur into the foot of the vine using a *pal*, or giant syringe. Then they tried sulpho-carbonate of potassium, which was deposited at the foot of each vine, but large quantities of water were needed to help this compound dissolve. Some of the larger Châteaux equiped themselves with proper pumping systems and set up a network of hoses designed to carry the water to the vines.

The *soissonnais* spray. Print from *Parcs et Jardins*, 1908. *(Private collection.)*

But in 1895 the real solution to the problem was found, and the practice of grafting the noble French grape varieties onto American rootstocks was finally adopted. The replanting process continued for several decades. In order to restore the weakened vines they were helped by generous doses of manure, as well as the first uses of chemical fertilisers.

Contrary to the common belief in England particularly, phylloxera did not destroy the Médoc vineyard. On the contrary, it led to increased production. So much so, that the merchants began to be alarmed. Neither was there any problem of depopulation. As production increased, so did the population of the area: wine workers, and those qualified to help treat the vines with sulphur poured into the region.

The second blow delivered to the quality and production of wines in the area came from mildew – a fact which is often ignored by writers who tend to concentrate on the devastating effects of phylloxera.

Mildew, or *Peronospora viticola*, first appeared in 1882 and had soon invaded all the vineyards. It did dreadful damage, killing off the foliage as well as the fruit of the vine and thus drastically reducing the harvests. What wines did survive were unbalanced, being acidic and musty to the taste and low in alcohol. Many wines deteriorated when they were bottled. One man came to the rescue: Alexis Millardet from the University of Bordeaux, in partnership with Ernest David, estate manager at Château Dauzac in Labarde and Château Ducru-Beaucaillou at Saint-Julien, discovered an efficient remedy: *bouillie bordelaise*, or Bordeaux mixture. Millardet's solution was a mixture of copper sulphate and lime, diluted in water and sprayed on the vine. Although this treatment protected the vines from mildew, it did not eliminate it. Mildew proved to be almost indestructible and remains a menace today. Spraying became common practice from 1885, but it was sometime before it had a widespread effect and by then much hardship had been caused to the wine growers. In 1886, because preventive treatments were still in their infancy, roughly half the *grands crus* harvest was lost altogether. Even hand spraying proved inadequate to always fight off mildew, attacks of which were particularly virulent during hot, humid weather – such as in 1910 and 1915. Faced with the twin foes of mildew and phylloxera, and with the threat of oidium ever present, the Médoc wine growers had learned to deal with adversity, but at a price. The increased costs of production coincided with small crops resulting from the deseased vines so that, at Palmer as elsewhere, from 1881 to 1890 crops were low, and financial results were poor.

❦ Stop the *pistrouillage*.

1890 marked a turning point in the quotations on all classed growths, including the *grands vins* of Palmer. A run of bad years had caused prices to collapse and the industry was ripe for fraud. Some took the easy way out and began the *pistrouillage* – a term created by Jouet, the manager of Château Latour, for the more outrageous degrees of blending that were put into practice. Rumours were rife in England, where "blended Clarets" were being offered.

Whilst rumours concerning the destruction of the Médoc vineyards by phylloxera were still circulating in England, production was in fact increasing dramatically. Between 1891 and 1900, Palmer produced an average of 152 tonneaux, an increase of 38 per cent on the previous decade. Three of those years (1893, 1896 and 1900) produced the unheard of total of over 200 tonneaux each.

"The terrible decade."

In Médoc, the expression "the terrible decade" generally refers to the first ten years of this century. During this time there was a general sense of an industry in disarray, pinpointed by Lawton who wrote that "sadly, quality is no longer an issue when people buy, low prices are what matter nowadays".

The Palmer harvest decreased again, to an average of only 125 tonneaux, only 87 per cent of the previous decade's average. Production varied from one extreme to another – in 1901, Palmer achieved a total of 250 tonneaux, while nine years later they could only muster 45. Prices collapsed – the average price for Palmer betwen 1901 and 1910 fell to only 72 per cent of the average for the previous decade, and for the period 1901 to 1906 was only 679 francs per tonneau. This gives a good idea of the depth of the crisis.

From 1907 to 1920, the wine growers were to some degree protected from disaster by the introduction of the *abonnements*, or subscriptions, which resulted in the merchants sharing in the risks of production by contracting to buy the next five or ten harvests at a prefixed price.

This restricted the liberty of growers but had the merit of

PREVIOUS PAGES

Château Palmer.
An original feature
of the main sitting
room : a window
as an overmantel,
above the fireplace.

The Pereire Saga

preventing prices from falling even further. Though much criti-cised during the *Belle Époque*, when all was going well, it was a system that also guaranteed a certain revenue, removed the risk of stocks of unsold wine accumulating in growers' cellars, and ultimately preserved those Châteaux from the financial ruin that faced others.

During the decade of 1910-20 production at Palmer fell a further 35 per cent, and averaged only 82 tonneaux. The largest crop was that of 1912, which reached 125 tonneaux. But prices were improving and made an average of 2,155 francs; no less than 2.7 times that of the previous decade. The gross income increa-sed as the harvests were reduced, so that the property's average yearly income of 169,850 francs, was 83 per cent better than during the previous period.

Palmer resumed its commercial independence in 1916, and if this apparently resulted in some better prices, it has to be remembered that there was strong inflation after World War I so part of this increase was only nominal.

The average price per tonneau between 1916 and 1920 was 3,160 francs and these five years brought in 70.7 per cent of the entire income for that decade.

❦ Palmer: wine of Kings.

Most Palmer wines were distributed by the Bordeaux trade to the rest of France, and particularly to Britain and north-west Europe. But occasionally Château owners sold privately and Palmer's most famous client was Claude Debussy, the composer. In October 1917, he paid 90 francs for 24 bottles of Palmer 1909, a mere 3.75 francs per bottle, which were delivered to his Paris address. This was a comparable price to most other Médoc *grands vins*. Some old menus from this period confirm that Palmer wines were being enjoyed at the best tables – the Chambre des Imprimeurs served Palmer 1831 along with

Château Filhot, Château Poujeaux and a Richebourg 1831, at a dinner held in Paris on 12 June 1883.

Twenty-one years later, the Amis de l'Eau-Forte enjoyed a case or two of Palmer 1908, together with Chablis *en carafe*, other Médocs and 1906 Pommard. But the grandest event must have been in 1886, when Palmer was served at a dinner held in London to celebrate the Coronation of the Prince of Wales. One course was accompanied by Roederer champagne, Carte Blanche 1874, another by Château Palmer-Margaux 1875. Palmer also appeared regularly on the wine lists of the London clubs, such as Brooks.

Claude Debussy, a distinguished client of Palmer, at the piano in 1893. *(Private collection.)*

❧ The Precious Book of Louis Mellet.

Thanks to the help of his grandson, it has been possible to consult the notebook of Louis Mellet, who was manager of the Palmer estate during the 1920s. This document describes in

Nº 3361

Paris, le 22 OCT. 1917   191

Livré à M. Claude Debussy

80 Avenue du B de B.

Paris

_____

24 Palmer 1909

Encaisser 90.

Claude Debussy

PREVIOUS PAGE
**Delivery note
for bottles of Palmer
for Claude Debussy.**
*(Collection Caves
Pétrissans.)*

detail the various plots of vines and the running of the vineyard during a third of a century.

In the 1920s, the Palmer property comprised 190 hectares of land, of which 123 hectares, divided into 286 plots, were planted with vines – a total of 942,000 vinestocks. It was the largest property in Cantenac-Margaux.

Most of the vines were cabernet sauvignon, whereas only about 3 per cent was planted with merlot – a surprisingly low figure when one remembers that the merlot grape had been introduced to the Médoc in 1825.

Palmer had not followed this trend, but instead had remained loyal to ancient vinestocks: the malbec and the petit verdot, whilst other plots were still often composed of a mixture of several different varieties.

It seems likely that as a result of the winemaking methods being used during the period 1890-1920 the wines being made at Palmer were more tanic and powerful than they are today. In addition to the red wines, Palmer, like its powerful neighbour, Château Margaux, also produced from 1923-25 a dry white wine.

Louis Mellet's book reveals the list of the team of vineyard workers at Palmer in 1920.

There were 22 altogether, amongst them Joseph and his son Pierre Chardon, the latter of whom had been born in Palmer in 1903, and was to become its estate manager in 1938, remaining in that post until his retirement, when he was in turn succeeded by his two sons, Claude and Yves. A fine example of the loyalty and devotion shown to Palmer by several generations of the same family.

In the meantime Mellet ran the Château well, keeping a close watch on his team of wine workers and benefiting from the Pereire family's generous investments in their vineyard. Members of the family visited the Château regularly.

❦ An uncertain future.

The post-war decade was relatively good – Prices remained at a good level, but cultivation costs rose steadily, average production slipped to only 75 tonneaux and if it was a bright period, it was one that could not last.

The crisis of the 1930s was to prove critical for Palmer's revenues. Already fragile, and in spite of some good years during the previous decade, the increasing production costs were to prove decisive. The decade started with the three bad vintages of 1930, 1931 and 1932 – all of which were badly affected by mildew. Together with the world economic depression, this caused prices to collapse. Lawton's appraisal of the 1932 wines was damning: "Small and rather mediocre. They do not have a bad taste, but are only between 8° and 9°. I wonder what we are going to do with them? This is a disastrous blow to the reputation of our wines; a tragedy to have such wretched wines sold under such illustrious labels." During the period up to 1938, and in spite of two vintages of good quality – 1934 and 1937 –

there remained no demand for the grands crus, many of which faced financial ruin. It also resulted in the creation of many cooperatives. A decree of 1935 accorded a subsidy of 1,200 francs per hectare for vines to be pulled up. In October of the same year Baron Philippe de Rothschild lamented the fate of Médoc in his harvest speech: "A wind of ruin blows across Gascony and Aquitaine. I think that we are witnessing the burial of our land." Palmer did not escape. In the sales document of the domain, dated the 29 April 1938 it was stated that "M. Pereire declares that the vines uprooted since 1931 carried no obligation to be replanted". In this depressing economic climate many Châteaux, deeply in debt, were for sale, but had great difficulty in finding possible buyers. Land values tumbled. In 1934, the 340 hectares of Larose-Trintaudon and Larose-Perganson at Saint-Laurent-de-Médoc were sold for the derisory price of 300,000 francs. As usual, M. Lawton pinpointed the most significant news in the wine trade, writing in April 1935 that "Château Haut-Brion was bought by Mr Clarence Dillon of the important Dillon Read Corporation in America for 2,350,000 francs. At the same time, we were offered the chance to buy the Cheval-Blanc property for 2,500,000 francs. No one wanted it."

The Thirties marked the start of an era dominated by precarious finances, and an uncertain future – circumstances that lasted right up until World War II. It is hardly surprising that, in 1938, the Pereire family felt compelled to sell their beautiful Château.

❦ Quality first.

Since the Thirties Palmer has enjoyed an impressive development. But before this could begin the decision had to be taken by a general meeting of the Société Pereire in Paris on 15 June 1937, to sell the property. The *Société* nominated two trustees

A. Frédérick E. Mähler.

– Andre Baruch-Levy and the manager Louis Mellet – to liquidate all the Pereire property in the Médoc.

The Bordeaux wine trade was naturally interested in the possibility of acquiring the many properties that had been forced onto the market at this time. Five joined forces in 1938 to form the Société du Château Palmer.

Fernand Ginestet, the head of a long-established négociant company in Bordeaux, who was eventually to acquire Château Margaux, Frédérick Mähler, founder of the Société Mähler-Besse and Co, and the firm Sichel and Co, represented by Joseph Kiefer were joined by two brothers, Édouard and Louis Miailhe, who managed vineyard properties and Landes forests. This consortium bought Palmer for 300,000 francs, a sum which, in itself, gives some indication of the general devaluation of the Médoc vineyards.

Today it is difficult to realise that at the time nobody was interested in buying top vineyards. The wine was selling badly, the series of bad vintages had shaken the market and few wanted to invest in properties that offered no return on capital. After the nobility of the 18th century that had created the great vineyard properties, after new wealth of industry and banking had developed the culture of highly personalised wines during the 19th century, the fall in land values opened the way to a new kind of owner – professional wine traders who grasped the challenge of an "orphaned" wine-growing culture that was in a very bad state.

On 19 July, the new owners of Palmer consolidated their purchase, by acquiring further plots of land at the Moulin of Issan, Regat-des-Combes, Guinot and Regat-des-Gardes. The following month they bought part of Château Desmirail in Margaux for 32,000 francs – a low price for a property that was classified as a *troisième cru classé*.

Little by little, through purchases and exchanges, the Société Civile de Palmer was reconstituting the heart of the former Pereire domain.

 # A constant evolution.

Over the next 40 years, the Société of Château Palmer underwent many transformations. In 1941, it became a *société civile*, and its capital was increased from 25,000 francs to 2,500,000 francs. Before this date, the *Société* had 50 shares at 500 francs: 25 shares belonged to Fernand Ginestet while the other four members held 10 each. But Ginestet had sold 6 shares, three to Henry Mähler-Besse and three to Sichel and Co so that the breakdown became: Fernand Ginestet, 19 shares, Sichel and Co, 13, Frédérick Mähler-Besse 10, Henry Mähler-Besse 3 and Société Miailhe Frères 10 shares. In 1950, the Société Civile de Château Palmer issued new shares, resulting in: Ginestet, owning 28 shares, Sichel and Co 26, Frédérick Mähler-Besse 20, Henry Mähler-Besse 6 and each the Miailhe brothers 10.

The following year, Louis Miailhe sold out of the *Société*, offering five shares to Henry Mähler-Besse and five to Sichel and Co. This sale was based on the price of 75,000 francs per share, or three times the previous nominal value, and now resulted in Ginestet holding 28 shares, Sichel and Co 31, Frédérick Mähler-

Besse 25, Edouard Miailhe 10, and Henry Mähler-Besse 6. In 1955, Fernand Ginestet's son, Pierre, sold the shares he had inherited in the company to the children of Frédérick Mähler-Besse so that between 1938 and 1955, the Mähler-Besse family became the majority shareholder, with 59 per cent of the shares. Sichel and Co were the second largest shareholders, while the

Henry Mähler-Besse.

Miailhe family retained 10 per cent of the capital. Since then the position has continued to evolve. The number of shares has been increased, in 1987 the Miailhe family sold their remaining shares to the other share holders, and the shares of the inheritance of Frédérick Mähler-Besse have passed to various members of his large family, and to their descendants. By 1972, the successors of the five original associates were proprietors of an estate composed of 45 hectares of vines, that in a valuation was described in the following terms:

"A well concentrated vineyard, planted exclusively with fine grape varieties: merlot, cabernet sauvignon, cabernet franc, petit verdot. The vines are set on the well exposed gravelly ridges that make up the plateau of Margaux." The vineyard surrounds the principle residence and its outbuildings, and produces a remarkable wine of exceptional finesse.

This owes not only to the nature of the soil and to its situation, but also to the old vines, of the best varieties. The average age of the vineyard, having been progressively regenerated, is between 20 and 25 years. The domain can be considered to now be in full production. Describing the Château, the report continued: "A fine, and most attractive stone residence, built in 1857 by the Pereire brothers, incorporating a small cone-shaped tower at each corner. Repairs have been regular and carried out with care." The details went on to describe the estate manager's house, the accomodation for the 13 workers, the cellars and the vat rooms which allow the wine to be made and stored in the best possible conditions. "The cellars are maintained at a constant temperature and are visited frequently by tourists." The value of the estate, the agents agreed, was enhanced by the fact that it was in perfect condition.

❦ The war years: difficult times.

But this renovation had been achieved over many years, from just before World War II to the early 1970s, during times that were often difficult, and with frequent setbacks. Between 1938 and 1949, the Miailhe brothers, who lived in Bordeaux, ran the property. One of their first decisions was to entrust the day to day management of the vineyard to M. Pierre Chardon, who thus succeeded M. Mellet. Having been born on the state in 1903, and having spent his life working in its vineyards, he was well qualified to manage both the vines and the wine making. Inevitably the war created its own problems for Palmer, not the least of which was the occupation of the château by German troops. They caused considerable damage, destroying furniture,

Allan Sichel.

NEXT PAGES
**In the old *cuvier*
destemming
was done by hand
until 1983.
Painting 20th Century.
(Private collection.)**

**Château Palmer.
Pruning the vines.**

tapestries paneling and floors, estimated in 1945 at nearly two million francs. It is clear from the beautifully executed graffiti left on the second floor walls that the troops were no happier to be there than Palmer was to have them there!

There was also a shortage of manpower, and such essentials as copper sulphate and sulphur became difficult to find. The Vichy government created a tax on *appellation contrôlée* wines and established a scale of prices of 100,000 francs per tonneau for *premiers grands crus* (first growths), 80,000 francs for second growths and 60,000 francs for the third growth. This economic meddling needlessly complicated the harvest negotiations and created a black market in *grands crus*. Even a vintage as exceptional the 1945, low in volume, high in quality and still drunk

with delight by connoisseurs today, was almost impossible to sell. It was not until the 1950s that there was some improvement.

During the 1950s there was a change in the Palmer management. The Miailhe brothers resigned, Frédérick Mähler-Besse's son-in-law, Jean Bouteiller, owner of Château Lanessan in Cussac, was nominated administrator of Palmer and remained as such until his early death in 1962. He was succeeded by his son, Bertrand, ensuring continuity in the Château management. The fundamental policy, around which shareholders and management base all their decisions, is one of rigour. Producing the best possible wine each vintage is the only thing that matters, and if necessary vats, or even whole crops, are unhesitatingly declassified if they are not

Message left on a wall by German troops, who occupied the Château during the war.
"Far from the battle, now in barracks, the soldier wants his reward: rest!
The 5th."

111

considered worthy of Palmer. Short term losses are accepted without question, in the interests of long term reputation.

❧ The Fifties a turning-point.

Jean Bouteiller achieved a great deal for Palmer, and left to those who succeeded him much to be proud of. He increased the area under vines by 31 per cent in twelve years, taking it from 22 to 29 hectares. He also improved the proportion of grape varieties, reducing merlot from the high 60 per cent level that it had reached under Miailhe management, to a more reasonable 47 per cent and thus establishing a more traditional balance. Many people believe that the character of a wine depends primarily on the variety of grape from which it is made. Peter Sichel rejects this, pointing out that "Bordeaux has a marginal climate for the production of red wine, and it is because the climate is relatively cool for red grape varieties that the fruit retains more complexity of flavour. Our different grape varieties are very close to each other, but the merlot ripens more easily than cabernet, so that in colder years (1977 and 1979 for example), merlot is better than cabernet. But merlot is also more sensitive to the weather at flowering time in May-June, so that a good part of the harvest could be lost if it is too cold or too humid at that time – as happened in 1984. In every case merlot produces fruitier and rounder wines than cabernet which gives them greater length, complexity and aging capacity. In Margaux, where the soil is gravelly and light, we also like to have 5 to 10 per cent of petit verdot grapes, so as to increase the colour, strength and structure of the wine. But it is not the grape that determines the character of the wine – it is the *terroir*, which means not only the soil but also the subsoil, the drainage, the lie of the land and the microclimate. In a year of good maturity, it is in fact often difficult to recognise the difference between the casks of different grape varieties."

During Jean Bouteiller's reign, Palmer entered an exceptional period in its history, well illustrated by the success of both the 1953 and 1955 vintages. The broker, Jean-Paul Gardère, wrote enthusiastically about 1955: "We had everything we could wish for: reasonable quantity, first class quality and a reputation, guaranteed." The wines of 1955, he said were "well-coloured, with an excellent bouquet, round and already very flattering. It is reminiscent of the 1952 vintage." Palmer produced 110 tonneaux – the largest crop of the decade 1951-1960.

The foundations of Palmer's excellent reputation today were laid by the often difficult decisions taken in the difficult post war years by Jean Bouteiller, Henry Mähler-Besse and Allan Sichel. In spite of the low prices those vintages were fetching, they were determined to sacrifice any idea of short term profit to the priority of quality. It showed courageous confidence in the future, at a time when even covering costs was a problem.

Ploughing of the vines by horses was the practice at Palmer until the 1960s.

NEXT PAGE
The Chardon "clan".

Bouteiller was responsible for production, while Mähler-Besse and Sichel concentrated on sales and finance – which included the need to make frequent cash advances to the *Société* in order to finance the running costs. It was the era of sales *sur souche* ("on the vine"), when many *grands crus* were obliged to sell part of their crop months before the wine was made in order to create the cash flow required to carry them through to the harvest.

This happened in 1961. The first sales were made in February of that year – seven months before the harvest. Prices were based on those of the previous vintage, which had been of no more than "mediocre quality". Many *grands crus* sold what they expected to be about a third of a their crop, but, following a late May frost during the flowering period and a long summer drought, the yields were so low that what would have been a

Château Palmer.
Harvesting
in the 1950s.

third of a normal harvest, now turned out be 100 per cent of a vintage of quite exceptional quality.

Thanks to the financing provided by Mähler-Besse and Sichel, Palmer did not have to resort to such sales *sur souche*, one happy consequence of which is that lucky dinner guests can still hope to be served a bottle of the fabulous 1961 Château Palmer!

Peter Sichel has personal memories of those years: "The first vintages I sold were the 1952 and 1953. Nearly all our sales in those days were in cask – our clients each did their own bottling. Prices were the equivalent of around 550 francs per hogshead of 225 litres – about 1.83 franc per bottle! But it was difficult to sell, and when I returned from a week travelling with an order for a hogshead or two I was congratulated! One of our regular customers was British Railways, who served half bottles of Château Palmer as their *vin de maison* in the restaurant cars!

Peter Sichel continues: "Post-war wines were generally believed not to be as well-structured as the great pre-war vintages. But this is not always true. 1953, for instance, was first considered a fine and agreeable wine but not likely to last long in bottle. It still seemed young in 1963: in 1973, to everyone's surprise, it was deemed superb, and it was still going strong in 1983. It is only during the last four or five years that it has shown signs of tiredness. The ageing capacity of the grands vins of Médoc – and Palmer in particular – has often been underestimated. It is not a powerful structure that gives them this capacity: it is balance."

Château Palmer.
Destemming by hand.

In the 1950s it was still an occasion for a customer or enthusiastic amateur to come to Bordeaux. Henry Mähler-Besse and Allan Sichel, had build a faithful clientele for Palmer – the former particularly in Holland, which had been the country of origin of his father, and the latter in Britain. He regularly drove customers down from England – often it was their first visit to Bordeaux. Such visits inevitably included lunch at Palmer. The menu prepared by Yvonne – Mme Pierre Chardon, whose kindness and devotion all concerned with Palmer so well remember – was simple, always the same, but always delicious and greatly appreciated: omelette, entrecote grilled on vine cuttings, chips, salade, cheese, followed by Mme Chardon's specialite: *crème caramel*.

In those days ther was still no mechanisation in the vineyards.

Château Palmer.
The old *cuvier*,
with its large
wooden vats.

Until the 1960s the
vines were still
sprayed by hand at
Château Palmer.

Even the crushing of the grapes was done by hand, on the table
that can still be seen in the reception room, together with many old
vineyard and cellar tools. Tractors were still unheard, and almost
unheard of. It was a hard life. The catastrophic frost of 1956 – so
bad that it destroyed some vine stocks completely, a very rare
occurrence – ushered in the second part of the decade. In 1957
there were more frosts, condemning that harvest also to be small.
They were to be the first of a series of small crops (see table p. 120).
Eventually, the improving world economic situation, a renewed of
interest in fine wine from the USA, and the two exceptional vintages of 1959 and 1961 combined to revitalise the market.

❦ Prosperity returns.

If the ground for Palmer's success was prepared in the Fifties, the
seeds were planted in the Sixties. This was mainly due to the

Pierre Chardon.

excellent quality of three memorable vintages: 1961, 1962 and 1966. The memory is still alive of those three harvests, characterised by their intense, almost black, colour and their heady perfume. They were powerful, rich and with great length and piercing finesse. But it was also due to the fact that in poor years – such as 1963 and 1968 – Palmer did not hesitate to declassify the whole crop, so there would be no such thing as a poor wine under a Palmer label. Very few *crus* were as courageous as this. At Palmer, it was agreed that if a particular wine did not express the character of the soil, or if a particular vintage was not worthy of the Palmer name, it must be declassed. The years between 1960 and 1970 marked the passage from difficult times towards prosperity.

Year	Production	Area in Production	Yield per hectare
1955	110 tx	22	45 hl/ha
1956	60	22	24,5
1957	43	22	17,6
1958	75	24	28
1959	100	24	37,5
1960	121	27	40
1961	35	27	11,7
1962	76	29	23,5

Turnover was three times the level at which it had been during the previous decade, the vineyard was increased in size, and average production rose to 120 tonneaux per year. Palmer's finances were healthy and the *Société* was well placed to make the most of the improved circumstances. Other *grands crus* were enjoying the same situation.

The broker, Gardère summed up the situation: "We should acknowldege the fact that properties are now in a stronger position than they have been for a long time, if not for ever. Visit cellars, evaluate the stocks that are held and the healthy bank balances resulting from the orders they are taking, and you will understand why they are solidly confident of their position."

Palmer was now recognised as being on an equal footing with the best second growths of the Médoc. Past difficulties seemed far behind as Palmer and the rest of Médoc entered the Seventies, and a new prosperous period in its three hundred year history.

❦ The Chardon saga.

Before accompanying Palmer into the 1970s and the prosperity that has followed, proper acknowledgment should be given to the important contribution by the Chardon family, now in its fourth generation on the estate. Pierre Chardon was also for many years mayor of Cantenac. He had brought to Palmer the same qualities he had bestowed on his town hall: competent and responsible leadership, dedication to the job and professional discretion.

In spite of all the difficulties of the times he did everything to maintain the quality and reputation of Palmer and its wines.

In January, 1961, Pierre Chardon had been promoted chevalier de la Légion d'honneur. Jean Bouteiller, who ran the Palmer estate, had written in 1959 to Senator Portmann in Bordeaux urging him to confer the honour on Pierre Chardon: "You know Chardon, mayor of Cantenac, and manager of Château Palmer, of which I am the administrator. I know that friends recommended several years ago that he should be awarded the Légion

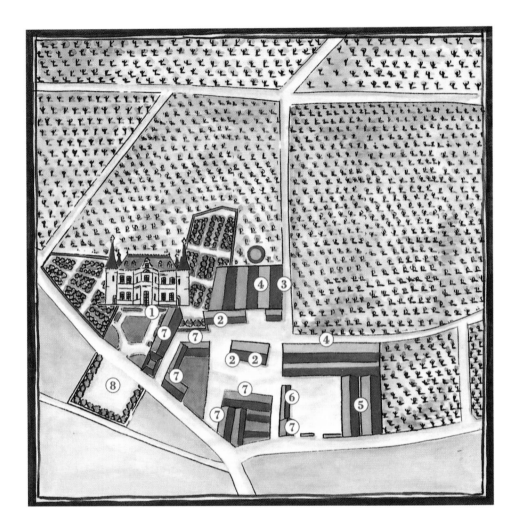

The Château Palmer
estate.
1. The Château
and park.
2. Visitors reception
and office.
3. Refectory for
the pickers.
4. Cellars.
5. *Cuvier* (vat house).
6. Garages.
7. Staff houses.
8. Parking area.
(Private collection.)

d'honneur. He has spent his life on the land, and has encouraged his two sons to do the same. He is totally devoted and with an attitude that has become rare this century. He is an excellent manager and a remarkable mayor, who fully deserves a very high reward. I thought it had already been arranged, and had been advised of the date of the ceremony, and then at the last moment it seems to have been blocked. I do not know by whom, but since then it has proved impossible to move the matter forward."

Jean Bouteiller asked the senator to intervene, adding "you can be certain that this high distinction would be well placed, much more so than in certain cases in the past".

Finally, it was with the help of Raymond Brun, senator of the Gironde, that Pierre Chardon eventually received the distinction of chevalier de la Légion d'honneur, from the hands of the minister of agriculture, M. Henri Rochereau. An award that reflected well on both Pierre Chardon, and Château Palmer.

Some years earlier Edouard Miailhe had also sung the praises of the Chardon family. In a memorandum of July 1956 he had written: "We have a family of great quality on the property, one who has worked faithfully for this estate for more than two generations. One cannot overestimate the value of such service and I think they should be recognised for it. We have a responsibility as shareholders to consider and organise the future of these men: M. Chardon, the father, Claude and Yves Chardon."

The shareholders responded. Claude Chardon has been a worthy successor to his father. His devotion to Palmer and his friendly welcome to visitors (as the author, who has known him well for a third of a century, can testify) have been great assets to the domain. Together with his brother, Yves, equally competent and loyal, they have, until their retirement in 1996, represented part of the soul of Palmer. They have been succeeded by Philippe Delfaut. The association continues into the next generation – Éric and Philippe, the sons of Yves and Claude respectively, also work at Palmer.

PREVIOUS PAGES
**The new *cuvier* of
Château Palmer:
a cathedral, to the
glory of wine.**

NEXT PAGE
TOP
**Label of the great
vintage of 1945.**

BELOW
**A porter,
with his hod.**

Of Wine and Men

❦ The Prosperity of Palmer: from the Seventies to the present.

Since the 1970s, Palmer, as the whole of the Médoc, has continued to consolidate its position. Despite the two small harvests
of 1971 and 1972 which unbalanced the market, causing artifi-
cially high prices, and then the oil crisis which led to a rise in
interest rates and a temporary collapse in prices, Palmer has
done well, thanks to a solidly built commercial policy, and in
spite of sometimes meagre profits. Though from 1978 costs
were covered, it was not until 1982 that it became truly viable.
After how many years of investment, effort and perseverance?

❦ The guardians of a *terroir*.

From 1970 to 1980, and since then, the development of the property can be described as prodigious. It is partly the result of
a specific commercial policy. The two negociant houses of
Sichel and Mähler-Besse organise the world wide distribution,
constantly travel to develop new markets, but at the same time
give priority to faithful, solidly based distributors. Also there is a
policy to retain part of the crop, so that it can be made available
to the market over a period, and as it matures.

1982 to 1996 have probably been the most prosperous years
in the Médoc's and in Palmer's history. – A strange paradox
in an era of fast-food and Coca-Cola, during part of which
interest rates were at a record level, and the world was in economic crisis.

How did it happen? No doubt a widening of the market – and a
market that has become more quality orientated. Where once
Britain, Belgium and the Netherlands had been the main destina-
tions of Palmer's wines, today Switzerland, USA, South America,
Japan, Scandinavia and Germany – to which must be now added
South West Asia – have also become important.

Fine Claret and White Bordeaux

London
Thursday, 16 May 1991 at 11.00 a.m.

CHRISTIE'S

PREVIOUS PAGE
**Cover of a Christie's
catalogue of 1991,
featuring
a photograph of
Château Palmer.**

Neither should one forget the French market – previously more interested in volume, but now it is quality that matters.

Allan Sichel died in 1965, when his son Peter took over the family seat in the Société Civile, as Franck Mähler-Besse and Bertrand Bouteiller have succeeded their fathers. The other shareholders are all descendants of Frédérick Mähler. More than shareholders they consider themselves to be the privileged guardians of an exceptional domain, and are resolute in their determination to continue with the same policies that created the success of their predecessors.

❧ Tangible results.

Betweeen 1970 and 1993, the area of cultivated land has increased by 36 per cent. The vineyard still covers the best *graves* of Cantenac-Margaux – the land which the Gascq family and General Palmer himself had originally cultivated. The Palmer vineyard has grown from 32 hectares in 1969 to 43 in 1990. The current proportion of grape varieties is 55 per cent cabernet sauvignon, 40 per cent merlot and 5 per cent petit verdot.

Through the 1980s and 1990s at Palmer, as elsewhere in the Médoc, the progress has been constant. The average production at Palmer has doubled compared to the 1970s, and in 1990s 308 tonneaux were made – the largest crop in Palmer's long history. But volume is never the priority, and there is never any hesitation to thin the crop in August whenever it seems that yield will be such that it could dilute the quality or the expression of character in the wine.

Only part of the harvest is sold under the main Château Palmer label. Another part, the second wine, is sold as Réserve du Général. This is a relatively new label, though the practice of only selecting the best vats to be sold under the main label is ancient, and goes back to the beginning of the XVIIIth century when "New French Claret" was first created. Until the Réserve

FINE CLARET
AND
WHITE BORDEAUX

The property of
Mähler-Besse, S.A., Bordeaux
and other trade and private owners

Including

Twenty-seven vintages of Château Palmer ranging from 1928 to 1987; an important collection from
an impeccable cellar in Bordeaux, including first growths of great vintages; many other private and
trade stocks, vintages 1961 to 1986, in lot sizes to interest all buyers; and dry and sweet white
Bordeaux.

Which will be sold at Christie's Great Rooms
on THURSDAY 16 MAY 1991
at 11.00 a.m. precisely

Tasting for catalogue subscribers and registered bidders with catalogues,
from 11.00 a.m. to 1 p.m. on Wednesday 15 May 1991,
at 8 King Street, St. James's, London S.W.1

In sending commissions or making enquiries, this sale should be referred to as
BESSE (4527)

Cover illustration:
M. Franck Mähler-Besse and M. Henry Mähler-Besse standing in the courtyard of Château Palmer

CHRISTIE, MANSON & WOODS LTD.
8 KING STREET, ST. JAMES'S, LONDON SW1Y 6QT

Telephone: 071-839 9060   Telex: 916429   Facsimile: 071-839 1611

Facsimile (Wine Department): 071-839 7869

Registered at the above address, No. 1128160

PREVIOUS PAGE

**Detail of the sale
of bottles of Palmer
at Christie's in 1991.**

Vintage Scene.

du Général label was created, declassified vats of Palmer were sold off simply as generic Margaux.

Though prices have certainly increased handsomely, so have production expenses. It currently costs about 200,000 francs per hectare to produce a great wine – eight to nine times more than it did in the 1960s. Wages and social security contributions account for 35 per cent to 40 per cent of the total. But there is also a heavy investment programme to be faced. It is this willingness to invest in the long term that has been the most fundamental element in the history of the *grands crus*, ever since they were first created in the XVIIIth century.

❦ Like a cathedral.

A good example of this policy of investment is to be found in the work that has been carried out at Palmer since 1993. The stone of all the buildings has been renovated, restoring to them the soft yellow tones of the original. A new entrance has been built, so that visitors may drive directly to the new reception

office, close to the cellars. The various installations for harvest time have been renewed: a modern kitchen and a refectory for the pickers, used also for receptions and banquets, have been built. Bertrand Bouteiller's office is now situated in another of the oldest buildings thoroughly renovated. But the most spectacular modernisation is the new *cuvier*, or vat room. Esthetically it is stunning – four rows of modern vats are surrounded by a pinewood gallery and roof that harmonises perfectly with the stainless steel, and seems to project the visitor into a cathedral, created to the glory of wine! An electronic control panel is all that can be seen of the complex computerised system that enables perfect control of the temperature of each individual vat, both during the alcoholic and the malolactic fermentations.

There is a total vat capacity of 5,000 hectolitres. Built by a local company, instead of being straight sided, as most stainless steel vats, they are slightly cone shaped, as were the old wooden vats,

**Claude Chardon
and Philippe Delfaut.**

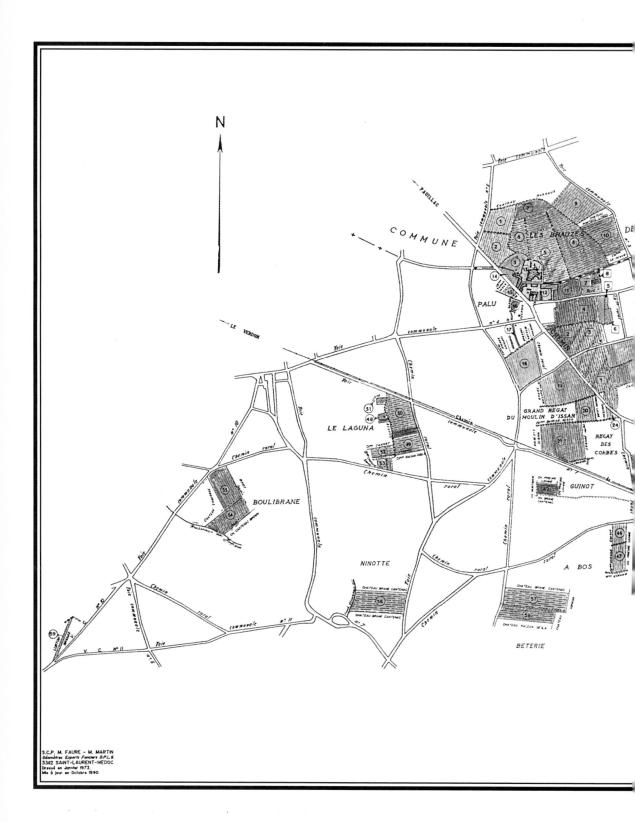

N

COMMUNE

LE VERDON

PALU

LES BRAUZES

LE LAGUNA

BOULIBRANE

GRAND REGAT
DU MOULIN D'ISSAN

REGAT
DES
COBBES

GUINOT

NINOTTE

A BOS

BETERIE

S.C.P. M. FAURE - M. MARTIN
Géomètres Experts Fonciers D.P.L.G.
3382 SAINT-LAURENT-MEDOC
Dressé en Janvier 1973.
Mis à jour en Octobre 1990.

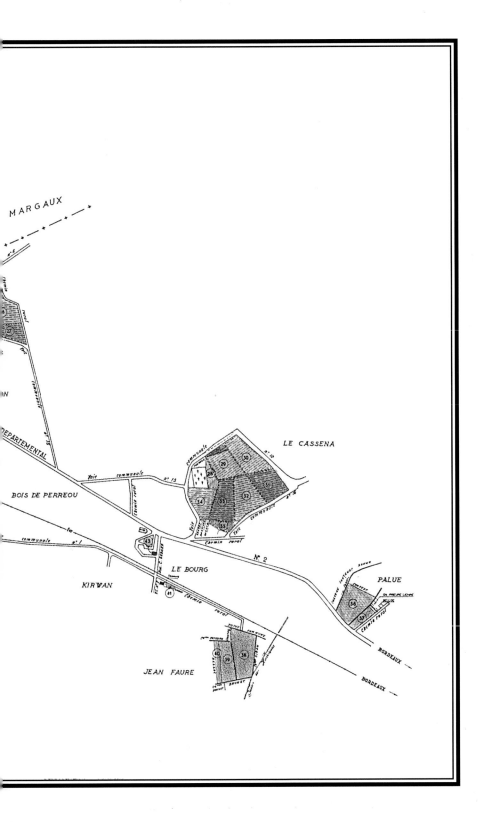

MARGAUX

DÉPARTEMENTAL

BOIS DE PERREOU

LE CASSENA

LE BOURG

KIRWAN

PALUE

JEAN FAURE

BORDEAUX

BORDEAUX

N° 2

LEFT
Plan of the different
plots of the Palmer
vineyard today.
Violet: merlot.
Orange: cabernet
sauvignon.
Blue: petit verdot.
Brown: not cultivated.
Pink: Château
and buildings.
Green: park.

NEXT PAGES
The grapes are
brought to the trailer,
where the quality
is checked, before
transfer
to the winery.

Château Palmer.
Controlling the quality
of the grapes.

so that the fermenting juice can circulate more effectively through the *chapeau* of skins to extract the maximum colour.

This new *cuvier* was used for the first time for the 1995 harvest. It was not without nostalgia that Palmer finally abandoned its old wooden vats, but it would have been wrong to ignore the advantages of modernisation. Stainless steel is easier to keep clean and to maintain in perfect condition. For a great vintage, Gardère wrote, you need "a *terroir* of quality, healthy grapes... and clean vats".

Palmer has modernised, but carefully and wisely: an evolution rather than a revolution. The objective has been the same as it has been since the estate was created – to produce a wine that fully expresses the finesse and the character of a great Margaux.

❦ "Wine evolves at its own pace..."

As we have seen at Palmer, quality always comes first – even at the cost of financial sacrifice. The proprietors refuse to automatically market even Réserve du Général every year, and will only sell wines under that label that are also worthy of the estate. Distributors are selected with the same care, to make sure that the wine reaches the right people. The wine is not just sold to the highest bidder. Ensuring as far as possible that there is always some stock available of older, mature vintages is another element of the policy. Certain vintages are destined to mature for more than fifty years so it is important to be able to taste such wines at their best. Great wine evolves at its own pace – so that too must be respected.

Palmer is a family affair, and not a financial trust. As generations have followed each other the partners have always been able to work well together, sharing the same priorities and the same objectives. They meet every month to discuss policy, and to take whatever decisions are necessary. The management is present on the ground. Constant vigilance is needed in a

Bertrand Bouteiller
(right)

Peter Sichel
(left).

Franck Mähler-Besse.

company that prides itself on the longevity of its product. Although the *Société* is more than willing to adapt to the modern age – as the installation of the stainless steel vats shows – it also determined to preserve the heritage of the past.

Last but not least, the human side of the business remains vital. Staff is valued for its contribution and everyone, client or not, is cheerfully welcomed to the estate. "We make a good wine, and we're proud of it" is the attitude of everyone concerned.

PREVIOUS PAGE
The technical director checking the density of the must.

ABOVE
Control panel for the fermentation temperatures. Each vat is individually computer monitored.

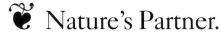 Nature's Partner.

Man cannot create a *grand vin* on his own and so, to be the owner of a *grand cru*, is to be in partnership with nature. As Peter Sichel describes it:

"The character of a wine originates from its *terroir*, as our own characters, and those of our children, depend on our genes. To create a *grand vin*, man must therefore respect the character of

the soil. A great wine is not one that has been dominated by
the wine maker, it is a wine in which man has been able to help
the *terroir* to express itself to the greatest advantage. But just
as the personality of man will vary depending on the environ-
ment in which he was brought up, so will that of a wine vary
from one year to another depending on the weather conditions
that prevailed that year. In a warm year the character will be
expressed generously, but perhaps with less elegance; in a cold
year it might appear closed up and reserved, but will develop
more complexity; in a wet year the expression of character
might be diluted – but it should always be present. Man's responsibility is to pick the grapes healthy and ripe, to allow
the natural fermentation to take place under the best possible
conditions, and to mercilessly eliminate from the blend any

PREVIOUS PAGE
**Château Palmer.
The new *cuvier*.
A blend of tradition
and efficiency.**

vat that does not satisfactorily express the character of the *terroir*. In a nutshell, it can be said that character comes from the *terroir*, personality from the weather conditions, but quality from human skill."

**Tasting under the
watchful eye of
Pey-Berland,
archbishop
of Bordeaux in 1440.**

PREVIOUS PAGES
**Château Palmer.
The barrel cellar
for the wine in
its second year.**

❦ The historical profile of Palmer is exemplary.

The Château has survived for almost three centuries. It has come through many difficulties and long periods of crisis. In fact, in all that time there have really only been three "golden ages" of real prosperity: a twenty year period in the second half of the XVIIIth century, about thirty years a century later, and the current era, that began in the 1980s.

At the end of it all there is a wine with a great reputation; known for its finesse, balance, elegance and complexities of floral flavours, and aromas.

There is an inimitable Palmer style and character that is fully expressed in such famous vintages as the fabulous 1961, which still lingers on in the minds of wine lovers. But other vintages also spring to mind: the powerful 1970, the delicacy of the 1971, the great 1975 and, from the last decade, the rich volume of the 1982, the length and elegance of the 1983, the fruit and charm of the 1985, the complexity of such maturing vintages as 1986, 1988, 1989 ad 1990.

Though each different they all express a harmonious partnership between man and his *terroir*. Thinking about the joy of tasting these great vintages makes it easy to forget the pleasure also to be found from lesser years! Somehow such wines make you forget all the worries and all the problems they occasioned – they can even be seen as a homage that the *terroir* is paying to man. Through the ages the owners of Palmer always seem to have understood their role: controlling yields, not hesitating to invest wisely in evolving techniques, learning from oenological and viticultural progress, selecting the right grape varieties, proper and moderate use of fertilisers, and discreetly promoting the image of their Château.

Not least of Palmer's merits is the way in which visitors are welcomed. The doors are always open to receive wine enthusiasts, and to help them learn more about the vineyard, and the fruit it

bears. It is not by chance that Palmer, classified a third growth in 1855, is now recognised by both professionals and amateurs from all over the world as equal to the best second growths: *Noblesse Oblige*.

Photos Credits

Photographs by
JEAN-PIERRE LAGIEWSKI

PRIVATE COLLECTION
P. 16, 17, 18, 19, 20, 21, 25, 26, 50, 56, 71, 74,
78, 79, 91, 97, 98, 101, 108-109, 122.

LAUROS-GIRAUDON, Paris
P. 22-23, 57, 67.

ROGER-VIOLLET, Paris
P. 70.

SYLVAIN PELLY, Paris
P. 56, 100.

RÉUNION DES MUSÉES NATIONAUX, Paris
P. 22-23.

Translated by

Carolyn Hart

Design and page layout by

Raymonde Branger.

Printed by

in 1997

for Éditions STOCK, Paris.